HIGHWAY TO HELL

The Armageddon Chronicles, 2015–2024

SCOTT RITTER

Foreword by
Larry Wilkerson

Clarity Press, Inc.

©2025 Scott Ritter

ISBN: 978-1-963892-20-8
EBOOK ISBN: 978-1-963892-21-5

In-house editor: Diana G. Collier
Interior typesetting & design: Becky Luening

ALL RIGHTS RESERVED: Except for purposes of review, this book may not be copied, or stored in any information retrieval system, in whole or in part, without permission in writing from the publishers.

Library of Congress Control Number: 2025934447

Clarity Press, Inc.
2625 Piedmont Rd. NE, Ste. 56
Atlanta, GA 30324, USA
https://www.claritypress.com

TABLE OF CONTENTS

Introduction vii

Foreword by Lawrence Wilkerson xi

Prologue: On a Highway to Hell xxi

Part One: The Arms Race, Part One
    Chapter One: Missiles without a Mission/Object 4202 3
    Chapter Two: Can You Hear Me Now? 16
    Chapter Three: Satan's Child 28
    Chapter Four: MAD no More 33

Part Two: The INF Treaty
    Chapter Five: Missile Madness 43
    Chapter Six: One Minute to Midnight 48
    Chapter Seven: The Death of a Treaty 59
    Chapter Eight: The Consequences of Failure 69

Part Three: New START
    Chapter Nine: Hope 77
    Chapter Ten: Have Your Cake and Eat it Too 82
    Chapter Eleven: No Start to New START 87
    Chapter Twelve: The Death of Arms Control 98

Part Four: China, North Korea, Iran and Israel
    Chapter Thirteen: Awaken the Dragon 111
    Chapter Fourteen: Escalate to Deescalate 117
    Chapter Fifteen: North Korea Goes Ballistic 121
    Chapter Sixteen: The Israeli-Iranian Nuclear Conundrum 131

Part Five: The Arms Race, Part Two
    Chapter Seventeen: Nuclear High Noon in Europe 145
    Chapter Eighteen: The Hobson's Choice 153
    Chapter Nineteen: Lowering the Threshold 165
    Chapter Twenty: The Growing Threat of Nuclear War 173

Conclusion: F*ck Them/72 Hours 186

INTRODUCTION

As this is being written, the world is coming face to face with an existential crisis of which most of humanity remains blissfully ignorant—the imminent threat of nuclear war. If ever there was a moment purpose built for a book, this is the moment, this is the war, and this is the book.

Some might look at a book comprised of a compendium of articles written over the span of a decade as the lazy man's way of chronicling such a subject. But when it comes to the issue of a potential nuclear Armageddon, I have concluded that it is more important to understand the journey of how we got to where we are, than it is to provide a snapshot of how things stand at the present.

Assembling articles that have been written over time enables the reader to relive the past by projecting them into the moment when the issues that resonate today actually occurred, examining the event not through backward glances, but rather fresh with the emotion that can only be felt as the event is experienced for the first time.

This helps readers to more readily discern the existential nature of the threat of a nuclear conflict that now seems conceivable than ever, as decisionmakers raise the option more frequently and the masses have become almost inured to the prospects of its horrors. This realization, however, is best achieved by taking the reader back in time to experience events as they occurred, as opposed to how they then became recorded in history. The rawness of the moment, comprised as it is of the freshness of the initial assessment combined with the brashness of related predictive analysis, is magnified by the insights gained through the passage of time.

Whereas there is a tendency for the chronicler of bad tidings to be characterized as "the boy who cried wolf" insofar as nothing has happened—*yet*. But looking back, and armed with the knowledge of how things play out, this provision of a harbinger of apocalypse might rather reclassify its author as a modern-day Cassandra. I have been extolling the dangers of nuclear war for more than a decade and lamenting the lack of effective arms control mechanism to bring this danger into check. And I have watched, dumbfounded, as events seem to take on a trajectory towards what may be their inevitable conclusion.

Highway to Hell: The Armageddon Chronicles captures my efforts to sound the alarm in this regard.

But this book is more than simply a platform for educating the reader about the danger of nuclear war.

It is also a manifesto in defense of free speech.

The U.S. government, working hand-in-glove with the American mainstream media, has strived to silence and/or suppress dissenting voices, especially those which provide a platform for ideas that effectively and authoritatively challenge the official narrative. The U.S. government has been seeking to silence me since 1998, when I resigned from the United Nations and began exposing the misinformation being spread about Iraqi weapons of mass destruction. When the *New York Times, Washington Post, Los Angeles Times, Boston Globe* and other big-name newspapers stopped publishing my writing, I was fortunate enough to be able to continue to publish my work online using so-called alternative media outlets.

The *Huffington Post, TruthDig, The Washington Spectator, The American Conservative, Consortium News,* and *Energy Intelligence* have all worked with me to get some of my best analysis published for the edification of a broad audience. Likewise, *Russia Today* and *Sputnik* similarly allowed me to publish articles that would be read by a global community. Over the years, pressure has been brought to bear to close my access to certain publishers, including the recent action by the U.S. government to prevent my continued contributions to *Russia Today* and *Sputnik*.

INTRODUCTION

By publishing my collective works on nuclear weapons, disarmament and arms control sourced from such a wide-range of publishers—some progressive, some conservative, others middle of the road, and some foreign-based—Clarity Press has helped create a testament to the integrity of both the author and publisher when it comes to the treatment of such complex and highly nuanced topics.

At the end of the day, there is no difference in content and style of the articles I wrote as they were published in the various outlets they appeared in. This, more than anything, underscores the legitimacy of the journalism involved—if one cannot discern the difference between the touch of a progressive editor from that of their conservative counterpart, and of an American editor from that of a Russian, that speaks volumes about the integrity of the product, and the purity of the motives underpinning their production.

In this regard, I wish to thank all of the editors who have assisted me over the years in bringing these articles, and all the others I have written, to the public eye.

Scott Ritter
Delmar, New York

FOREWORD

Being asked to compose a foreword for a book about nuclear weapons is like being asked to write about man's fate. And I don't mean as André Malraux described that fate so superbly in a work of that very name in its usual English-translated title—or, then again, perhaps I do, with a twist, a diabolical, human-race-killing twist. ["What is Man?" Malraux asks. "A miserable little pile of secrets...," he answers, and it goes downhill from there.]

Alongside the burgeoning crisis of the climate, nuclear weapons threaten seriously the very existence of the human race—that is, nuclear extinction may be humanity's ultimate fate. That has never been so before through the entire five millennia of human existence about which we know something, from a little to a lot—the latter abundance beginning about 3,000 years ago and growing as we move into modernity.

Over those better-known 3,000 years there were hundreds of empires, huge, large, medium and small. There were even tiny, would-be aspirants such as the Israelites of whom the prophet Jeremiah repeatedly predicted the demise, as one might rightfully contend similar modern prophets—such as the author of this book—are predicting the demise of the latest iteration of the Israelites, the modern statelet of Israel. In 587BC, the Army of Babylon, as Jeremiah foresaw, utterly devastated the Israelites. After a siege of more than a year, Jerusalem was totally destroyed along with Solomon's Temple, much as Jeremiah had foretold.

In the scheme of human existence, however, such tiny enclaves were insignificant when compared to the imperial giants in which these smaller enclaves had to exist: the Persian Empire—some would contend the most powerful of all—the Mongol Empire, the Mughal Empire, the Western and then the Eastern (Byzantine) Roman Empires, the Ottoman, the Russian, the French, the Spanish, and perhaps the most geographically encompassing of all—upon whose realm it was said the sun never set—the British Empire; and a multitude of others of lesser scope and power, including more recently the Austro-Hungarian, the war-forged empires of the Third Reich and Tojo's Imperial Japan. All came and went, some, like Hitler's and Tojo's, blindingly fast in historical-imperial terms.

Regardless of size and reach, power and wealth, all disappeared. None of the old ones are with us today, in spite of a few rulers' wistful desires. But today there is of course an upstart: the American Empire, marking its beginning in 1945. One could argue effectively that with more than 750 military installations scattered all across the globe, with that globe divided into military fiefdoms, with a world-spanning financial, economic, and trade structure fashioned largely by that Empire, and with better than a quarter of the almost nine billion people in the world under its imperial sanctions at any given moment, the reach of the American Empire is indeed awesome.

But there is something else, something quite unique and quite disturbing. No other empire in all of human history ever achieved what the American Empire has achieved. Not in 50,000 years of certain "human" existence. Not in the 5,000 years we know something about. Not in the 3,000 we have studied and chronicled amazingly well. *No empire ever invented the technological capacity to destroy the human race.*

Until America. Whether Robert Oppenheimer, the father of the atomic bomb, actually uttered the words or not is irrelevant; the Indian scripture does record them: "Now I am become Death, the Destroyer of Worlds." Most likely these are some of the most well-known words of the *Bhagavad Gita*—and despite some religious scholars' opinions to the contrary, very appropriate to the world's present situation, even in its religious context.

FOREWORD

Through its Manhattan Project, America invented the means to destroy every human life on earth and much else. It is of little consequence that if we had not done so someone else would have—Hitler, Stalin, some later tyrant—but it is not a provable assertion no matter how morally justifying the current Empire might find it. *A supposed liberal democracy called the United States of America did do it. And then used these weapons in war to murder more than a hundred and fifty thousand of its enemies.*

More significantly—particularly if we accept the assertion above that if America had not done it someone else would have—that same liberal democracy thwarted every meaningful effort to attempt to manage the monstrosity it had created through international mechanisms, even though such notable wartime champions as Five-Star General Dwight Eisenhower favored such efforts. Ironically enough, sole ownership of "the Destroyer of Worlds" lasted only four years and a month-plus. So much for military secrecy as opposed to international cooperation and diplomacy.

And so here we are, along with every other member of the human race. No one can escape it.

This book gives the reader ample reason—horribly frightening reason—to believe that, like Jeremiah's Israelites, we have run the course and done so oblivious to our own "Jeremiahs"—courageous patriots like Dan Ellsberg, for instance, and the author of this book.

I knew Dan for the last decade or so of his truly remarkable and valuable existence. Perhaps no one had the singular impact that Dan did when it came to exposing the Empire's dirty secrets. And I know that were he still with us, Scott Ritter would have had him write this foreword and not me and if Scott asked me my view I would have said, absolutely it should be Dan. But I will also say that Scott Ritter stands sharply in the shadow of Dan and with this book the full sunlight strikes them both.

Of course, there are others as well; in fact, the true patriots—not of the Empire necessarily but of the entire human race—are legion and all over the globe. But theirs is not the power of Empire; it is the very limited but real power of humanity. And there alone is a reason to condemn the Empire because its aim is to thwart humanity at every juncture. In fact, that is its aim as surely as, in a more immediate sense, its aim was—perhaps still is—to destroy the lives of students, professors, and university officials all across the United States who had the gall and the guts to protest the genocide occurring in Gaza and on the West Bank.

Much additional reason to join the real "patriots of humanity" is contained in this volume by Scott Ritter.

For instance, Ritter examines the sheer lunacy of what is most definitely now a renewed nuclear arms race, with even China defying Mao Tse-Tung's long-lived belief and doctrine that nuclear weapons were an abomination and so China would only build sufficient numbers to deter the other insane leaders in the world. Instead, China is embarked today on a major build-out of its nuclear weapons complex, sufficient to ride out a first strike and retaliate devastatingly.

The cause of Beijing's decision lies directly at the feet of the American Empire, and particularly its single-handed abrogation of every nuclear weapons treaty the Cold War produced, from the absolutely insane decision by President George W. Bush to depart from—and thus abrogate—the Anti-Ballistic Missile Treaty, to the New START treaty process which no one in his right mind would expect President Vladimir Putin to want to continue with an Empire he considers totally deceitful and unreliable. At one point, Ritter characterizes today's U.S. negotiating technique thusly: "The U.S. wants Russia and China to rein in their respective strategic nuclear arsenals while it modernizes its own nuclear defenses at the same time. When it comes to strategic nukes, the U.S. can't have its cake and eat it too."

But, as he goes on to illustrate, that is precisely what the Empire is planning.

A most dangerous case in point is that the Empire's abrogation of nuclear weapons treaties included, as the author describes, the INF treaty that rid the world of an entire class of nuclear weapons—arguably the most dangerous class because these weapons are the most likely to be used in anger and lead to a more general exchange. Think Ukraine and Gaza, for current examples of such "anger."

The INF Treaty—as chairman of the Joint Chiefs of Staff and, later, Secretary of State Colin Powell told me more than once while wearing both his military hat and his diplomatic one—was one of America's singular diplomatic achievements and he was duly proud of having been a part of its creation, first as Deputy National Security Advisor and then, when his superior Frank Carlucci moved to be Secretary of Defense, as National Security Advisor to President Ronald Reagan.

Ritter lays out for all to read the depth and breadth of the imperial lunacy of summarily departing these effective treaty regimes. In fact, he points out, the world does not even have left the near-insanity of the Cold War-developed deterrence theory of Mutual Assured Destruction, or "MAD," whose near-insanity is illustrated so brilliantly in Stanley Kubrick's 1964 movie *Dr. Strangelove or: How I Learned to Stop Worrying and Love the Bomb*.

MIT Professor Emeritus Dr. Ted Postol's detailed discussion of the Empire's present development of missile warhead technology illuminates its awesomely frightening prospects clearly. Briefly, and assuredly inexpertly, as I understand Dr. Postol we are engineering MIRVs (Multiple Independently Targetable Reentry Vehicles) to have such incredible accuracy that, unlike with previous technology, warhead fratricide and "near-misses" will be eliminated. In short, every one of the colossally destructive warheads—usually 8–10 in a single missile's nosecone—will "land on target." This affords a decisive first-strike capability where one did not previously exist, and presents an invitation to launch pre-emptively and thus, Saints forbid, initiate a nuclear holocaust intentionally, believing our side will "win," utilizing the so-called "first-strike option." It is sheer insanity.

Ritter also covers the dangerous and ongoing Russian nuclear doctrinal developments, including the so-called "nuclear de-escalation" doctrine, which rivals MAD for near-insanity. However, as a military professional for 31 years I can completely understand the Russian fears that generated such a doctrine. Fears of the duplicity, the lies, and the outright skullduggery of the Empire with regard to its treaty abandonments and its reaction to the prospect of its imminent defeat in the war in Ukraine. And, lest we forget, the imperial perfidy in Georgia years before and, sad to report, today as well. In 2004, the president I served, George W. Bush, actually stood beside his counterpart in Tbilisi, Georgia's President Mikheil Saakashvili, and publicly announced that Georgia would be a member of the NATO Alliance. Russia showed almost immediately what that meant by initiating military action against Georgia. Nonetheless, Russia's nuclear de-escalation is an acutely dangerous doctrine, one calling primarily upon that class of nuclear weapons once eliminated by the INF Treaty the Empire so cavalierly and deceitfully discarded.

Ritter also covers the near-pariah state whose nuclear negotiators and nuclear policies I knew quite well from 2002–2005, as Secretary of State Powell assigned me key responsibilities as his chief of staff in dealing with Pyongyang. From Kang Sok-Ju to Lee Gun to the head man himself, Kim Jong-il, we labored in the nuclear trenches, so to speak, to persuade the North Koreans to cease their pursuit of a nuclear weapon capability. This, only to be shocked as we finally got past Vice President Richard Cheney's constant obstructions and were able to meet directly with the DPRK's nuclear negotiators in

Pyongyang—and I think it's fair to say they shocked our Assistant Secretary, Jim Kelly, when they readily admitted they already possessed nuclear weapons! So much for Cheney's previous objections to and interruptions of our tireless diplomatic efforts he always stymied . We were, in a phrase, too late.

And then there is that tiny statelet at the eastern end of the Mediterranean Sea led by a modern-day barbarian named Benjamin Netanyahu, Israel. There are anywhere from 100–200 nuclear weapons, probably at Dimona and elsewhere, that according to most rational thinking should never have gotten to Israel in the first place. Thank the feckless Empire once again. With presidential knowledge, the Empire gave to Israel the wherewithal to construct those weapons.

Ritter points out how dangerous this situation truly is. I recently asked a colleague if he really considered that Netanyahu, were he personally imperiled due to an apparent existential situation into which he had led Israel, would hesitate to reach for the ultimate solution. He considered the question for a moment or two and then said, "No, actually." Pausing briefly, he then added: "And I would not blame him."

Continuing our conversation, now grown utterly unimaginable to me, I asked: "And why do you arrive at that conclusion?"

"Because it's his watch, he concludes Israel is fatally imperiled, and he has no other choice."

I responded: "I suppose Nebuchadnezzar in Babylon, were he transplanted to modern times, would say, 'I'm certainly happy that no such arsenal existed when my armies sacked the Temple and destroyed and enslaved the Israelites.'"

"And your point is?" my colleague asked, a quizzical look in his eyes.

"Simple and not so simple," I said. "The entire Babylonian Empire despite its power might have disappeared, a chain reaction might have been initiated, and the rest of the world go with it."

"That's hardly likely," he responded.

"Perhaps, but you're prepared to wager the world on that conjecture? And before you reply, tell me also who gave Bibi the right to make such a decision."

He mused a moment, then said, with remarkable succinctness, "Well, his Sugar Daddy, America."

Scott Ritter in this book gives you all the detail you need to know that my colleague's insouciant nuclear response presumption is writ large across key regions of the world and not simply in the Levant. The light it sheds on the prevailing mentality is too damned accurate for comfort.

But there's more. The late Alan Hart, a friend of Israel's then-Prime Minister Golda Meir—when he worked for the BBC, he sent her three dozen red roses whenever he traveled to Israel—was invited often to have the very first interview with her when events were heating up. On one such occasion, they talked telephonically at length. She thanked him for the red roses he had just sent, told him that under the then-difficult circumstances she had to give her first interview to the Americans, but went on to reveal a deep truth to him. He wrote about this conversation with her in *WordPress's* 20 April 2016 "Palestine and Zionism: The Whole Truth":

"Even if the day comes," Hart wrote, "when the governments of the major powers are prepared to confront Zionism it could not be taken for granted that Israel's leaders would say: 'Okay. We'll do what you want.'"

"My reason for saying that," he continued, "is a statement Prime Minister Golda Meir made to me in one of my interviews with her for the BBC's Panorama programme in 1972. At one point I said to her, 'Prime Minister, I want to be sure I understand what you have just said.... You did mean that in a doomsday situation Israel would be prepared to take the region and the world down with it?'

FOREWORD

"Without a pause for reflection Golda replied: 'Yes. That's exactly what I'm saying.'"

Hart concluded, "That interview was broadcast on BBC 1 at eight o'clock on a Monday evening. An hour later *The Times* of London, then a seriously good newspaper, changed its lead editorial to quote what Golda said to me. It then added its own opinion – '*We had better believe her.*'" [italics mine]

Indeed. We—the world—had better believe her, and this book. Read it to see clearly why.

Lawrence Wilkerson
Retired U.S. Army Colonel and former Chief of Staff to Colin Powell
December 2024

PROLOGUE
On a Highway to Hell

Nuclear weapons offer an illusion of security. By allowing the U.S. nuclear posture to shift from deterrence to employment, there will be a scenario where the U.S. will use nuclear weapons. And then it's lights out.

Successive U.S. administrations have eschewed arms control in favor of maintaining American strategic advantage over real and/or imagined adversaries.

This is accomplished by embracing nuclear weapons employment strategies that deviate from simple deterrence into war-fighting at every level of conflict, including scenarios that don't involve a nuclear threat.

At a time when the U.S. advocates policies exacerbating already high levels of tension with nuclear-armed adversaries Russia and China, the Biden administration has signed off on a new nuclear employment plan that increases, rather that decreases, the probability of nuclear conflict.

Left unchecked, this policy can have only one possible outcome—total nuclear annihilation of humanity and the world we live in.

An interesting thing happened on the road to Armageddon.

In January 2017, then–Vice President Joe Biden, speaking at the Carnegie Endowment for International Peace, warned about the dangers inherent in expanding funding for, and by extension increasing the importance of, nuclear weapons.

"If future budgets reverse the choices we've made, and pour additional money into a nuclear buildup," said Biden—referring to Obama administration policies that included securing the New START

Treaty limiting the size of the U.S. and Russian nuclear arsenals—"it hearkens back to the Cold War and will do nothing to increase the day-to-day security of the United States or our allies."

Later, in 2019, Biden, now a candidate for president, commented on the decision made by President Donald Trump to deploy two missile systems—a cruise missile still under development, and the Trident submarine-launched ballistic missile deployed onboard the U.S. Navy's Ohio-class submarines—armed with a new low-yield nuclear warhead.

"The United States does not need new nuclear weapons," Biden declared in a written answer to questions posed by the Council for a Livable World. "Our current arsenal of weapons…is sufficient to meet our deterrence and alliance requirements."

In an article published in the March/April 2020 issue of *Foreign Affairs*, candidate Biden vowed to "renew our commitment to arms control for a new era," including a pledge to "pursue an extension of the New START treaty, an anchor of strategic stability between the United States and Russia and use that as a foundation for new arms control arrangements."

Biden went on to declare that "that the sole purpose of the U.S. nuclear arsenal should be deterring—and, if necessary, retaliating against—a nuclear attack. As president, I will work to put that belief into practice, in consultation with the U.S. military and U.S. allies."

Biden prevailed over Trump in the 2020 Presidential election, and on Jan. 21, 2021, was sworn in as the 46th President of the United States.

And then…nothing.

In March 2022, after much speculation about whether or not Biden would follow through with his pledge to implement a "sole purpose" nuclear policy, the Biden administration published the 2022 edition of the Nuclear Posture Review (NPR), a Congressionally mandated document which describes the United States nuclear strategy, policy, posture, and forces in support of the National Security Strategy (NSS) and National Defense Strategy (NDS).

It was a near carbon-copy of the February 2018 NPR published by the Trump administration, including language which enshrined as doctrine the U.S. ability to use nuclear weapons pre-emptively, even in scenarios that did not involve a nuclear threat.

In December 2022, during a reunion of personnel involved in the negotiation and implementation of the landmark 1987 Intermediate Nuclear Forces treaty, a senior Biden administration arms control official was asked by a veteran arms controller why Biden had backed away from his pledge regarding the "sole purpose" doctrine.

"The inter-agency wasn't ready for it," this official replied.

The "inter-agency" the official was referring to is the amalgam of departments and agencies, staffed by unelected career civil servants and military professionals who serve as the executioners of policy regarding America's nuclear enterprise.

It was a surprising, and extremely disappointing, admission on the part of an official whose oath of office binds them to the bedrock constitutional principle of executive authority and civilian control of the military.

Biden had, even before being sworn in, received push-back regarding any alterations in the nuclear doctrine of the United States.

In September 2020, Admiral Charles Richard, commander of U.S. Strategic Command responsible for America's nuclear arsenal, warned that, "We are on a trajectory, for the first time in our nation's history, to face two peer nuclear-capable competitors." Richard was referring to the nuclear arsenals of Russia and China.

Once he became president, Biden was immediately confronted with two major challenges for which he was ill-equipped to handle—the

Russia-Ukraine crisis, and China's assertion of its national interests over Taiwan and the South China Sea.

Both involved the potential of military escalation leading up to direct force-on-force conflict between the U.S. military and their Russian and Chinese counterparts, both of which included the possibility of nuclear war.

The Russian initiation of its "Special Military Operation" against Ukraine in February 2022 brought with it the inherent risk of escalation with NATO, leading to Russian threats about the potential for nuclear weapons use if NATO decided to directly intervene in Ukraine.

And a November 2022 Pentagon report forecast that China would increase its nuclear arsenal from around 400 weapons to more than 1,500 by 2035.

The New START treaty limits the number of deployed nuclear warheads to 1,550 each for the U.S. and Russia. The treaty was negotiated on the principle of bilateral reciprocity.

With the U.S. facing a potential Chinese nuclear arsenal of 1,500 weapons, and the existing Russian arsenal of around the same, it was clear that, left unchecked, the U.S. was going to find itself in a disadvantageous position when it came to its strategic nuclear forces.

While the NPR provides a general policy statement regarding the U.S. nuclear arsenal, there are two more documents—the President's Nuclear Employment Guidance and the Secretary of Defense's Nuclear Weapons Employment Planning and Posture Guidance—that direct planning for actual employment of nuclear weapons consistent with national policy.

The last Nuclear Employment Guidance document, published in 2019, was responsive to the 2018 NPR. This guidance fully incorporated the new low-yield W-76-2 nuclear warhead into the nuclear employment plans of the United States. It did the same for the new generation of B-61 gravity bombs that constitute NATO's nuclear deterrence force.

The employment plans were based upon the concept of "escalate to de-escalate" (i.e. by using a small nuclear weapon, the U.S. and NATO would deter Russia from escalating out of fear of bringing on a general nuclear exchange.)

In short, America's nuclear war plans were front-loaded for the localized employment of nuclear weapons against both a Russian and Chinese threat.

This U.S. nuclear war plan was premised on the ability to deter Russian nuclear escalation and not just deter but even defeat China's nuclear force using the number of nuclear warheads permitted under the caps implemented by the New START treaty.

However, the Biden administration is now confronted with the possibility and/or probability of a much larger, more capable Chinese strategic nuclear force able to survive a limited U.S. first-strike and deliver a nation-killing nuclear payload to U.S. soil in retaliation.

To adjust to this new reality, the U.S. would need to allocate nuclear warheads currently targeted against Russia onto China. This would require that the U.S. not only develop revised target lists for both Russia and China, but also rethink its targeting strategies in general, looking to maximize physical destruction over political impact.

More dangerously, the U.S. would have to look at employment strategies that maximized the element of surprise to ensure all targets were hit by their designated weapons. This would require a change in the readiness posture and operational deployment areas of U.S. nuclear forces.

With increased readiness comes the need for vigilance against any preemption efforts by any potential nuclear adversary, meaning that U.S. nuclear forces will be placed on a higher alert status.

In short, the risk of nuclear war, inadvertent, preemptive or in retaliation, has become exponentially greater.

In March the Biden administration reportedly issued a new Nuclear Employment Guidance document reflecting this reality.

Nowhere in this guidance is there consideration for using arms control as a means of managing the nuclear equation, either by extending the New START treaty, or working with China to prevent a Chinese nuclear breakout.

Instead, the U.S. appears to be more concerned about the erosion of nuclear deterrence that will be brought about by its diversion of weapons dedicated to address non-Chinese contingencies. Seeing the matter in this light, its answer to the problem is more, not fewer, nuclear weapons.

This is why the U.S. is going to let the New START treaty lapse in February 2026—once the treaty goes away, so, too, does the cap on the number of deployed warheads, enabling the U.S. nuclear establishment to further build up the U.S. operational nuclear arsenal so that there are enough weapons for every designated target.

The world is becoming a very dangerous place.

Nuclear weapons only offer the illusion of security.

By allowing the U.S. nuclear posture to shift away from deterrence toward warfighting, this will guarantee that eventually there will be a warfighting scenario where the U.S. will end up using nuclear weapons.

And then we all die.

We are, literally, on a Highway to Hell.

Scott Ritter

[This article was originally published by *Consortium News* on September 1, 2024]

PART ONE

The Arms Race, Part One

CHAPTER ONE
Missiles without a Mission/Object 4202

Retired General James Cartwright, who led U.S. Strategic Command responsible for America's strategic nuclear forces from 2004 until 2007, recently articulated in an interview that in order to safeguard American Minuteman III intercontinental ballistic missiles (ICBMs) from the threat of cyber-attack, the United States should "de-alert" them. How? By taking them "off-line" so that rather than being prepared to launch them at a moment's notice, it would take us 24 to 72 hours to get the missiles ready for operation. General Cartwright served as the lead author for a report issued last month by the Global Zero Commission favoring a gradual "de-alerting" by both the U.S. and Russia of their respective missile forces. But "de-alerting" American (and Russian) ICBMs only sidesteps the real question at hand: what is the mission of these missiles to begin with, and are they still needed today?

The Minuteman force has, for more than five decades, stood watch as the mainstay of American nuclear deterrence against the threat posed by hostile nuclear weapons. There were once 1,000 Minuteman missiles based in heavily reinforced underground silos scattered across the northern plains states. At present, there are 450 Minuteman III missiles deployed at three bases in North Dakota, Montana and Wyoming, with that number soon scheduled to be pared down to 400. The Minuteman III of today has little in common with the one that entered service in the 1970s. Significant service life extension programs, costing billions of dollars, have made the Minuteman

III viable as a weapons system through 2030, at which time it will need to be replaced.

But the Cold War that spawned the Minuteman III is long gone, and with it the need for the United States to maintain an aging fleet of missiles designed to survive a surprise Soviet nuclear attack. The costs of maintaining this relic of the Cold War is too great, and the benefit of retaining it too small.

Building a new missile, like extending the life of an old one, does not come cheap. The Congressional Budget Office has estimated the cost for such an enterprise to be $10 billion spread out between 2014 and 2023. A RAND study predicts a higher range, between $60 billion and $219 billion over a similar time frame. In this day and age of budget austerity where painful decisions are being made about overall defense force structure, spending this kind of money on a missile system whose mission ended two decades ago is the height of fiscal irresponsibility.

The Minuteman missile was once a critical component of a so-called nuclear triad composed of land-based ICBMs, nuclear-armed bombers, and submarine-launched ballistic missiles. The value of the Minuteman III to the triad today centers on the fact that any potential enemy would have to employ hundreds, if not thousands, of nuclear weapons to neutralize it—in short, the Minuteman III exists to serve as a nuclear sump in a world where the risk of massive nuclear attack is slim to none. It is this sort of mind-numbing reality that has led to professional atrophy within the ranks of the U.S. Air Force personnel who man the Minuteman III launch control centers, resulting in flagging morale, lax accountability and cheating scandals.

Nuclear deterrence today is not what it was thirty years ago. The Minuteman's raison d'être was always survivability against a Soviet nuclear attack. In the post-Soviet era, Russia has emerged as the preeminent nuclear challenger to the United States. But the Russian

Chapter One: *Missiles without a Mission/Object 4202*

strategic nuclear force is but a shadow of its Soviet predecessor. The threat of a Russian nuclear surprise attack today is minimal, and ably deterred by the U.S. Navy's Trident submarine missile force.

Not only that, the inability of the Minuteman III to respond to anything but a massive nuclear attack further reduces its viability as a weapon system capable of implementing the nuclear strategy of the United States today, where quick-reaction, short-duration nuclear contingencies favor the kind of operational flexibility offered by manned bombers and submarines.

Rather than being the force of stability it once was, the Minuteman III has become a destabilizing presence—any use of the missile, whether against North Korea, Iran or other so-called rogue state or non-state players, would likely trigger a "launch on detect" response from Russia or China (or both).

Its inherent first-strike capability has bred new generations of Russian and Chinese missiles designed solely to target the Minuteman III in its silos, increasing the possibility of inadvertent nuclear conflict rather than diminishing it.

The inescapable fact is that the Minuteman III today is a missile without a mission whose continued operational deployment represents neither sound military doctrine nor responsible fiscal policy—whether or not the missiles are "de-alerted." The realities associated with current and projected defense expenditures dictate that eventually the Minuteman III will find its way to the budgetary chopping block. It would be better for all involved that this decision be made now, before many billions of dollars are needlessly expended on a weapons system with no viable future. America's national security deserves nothing less.

• • •

Sometime soon, President-elect Trump will be briefed on the American plan for nuclear war, including the role he would play in ordering a launch. John F. Kennedy was the first American president briefed on this plan back in 1961. Afterwards, a shaken Kennedy told his secretary of state, Dean Rusk, "And we call ourselves the human race."

President Nixon was similarly appalled. "No matter what we do," he told his National Security Council, "they [the Soviets] lose their cities...what a decision." Ninety million Soviets would die in an American nuclear strike, Nixon was told. And 90 million Americans would die in a Soviet retaliation. And there was no way to change that outcome.

Nixon tried. He ordered the Pentagon to develop flexible nuclear responses to allow the United States the ability to "limit" nuclear conflict. President Carter did the same. In the end, however, the "game theory" rationalizations of thermonuclear warfare left the nation's leader faced with the reality of a Hobson's choice, where the only solution offered was global destruction.

Ronald Reagan flirted with the notion of "winnable" nuclear war, before recognizing the reality that there was no way to put the nuclear genie back in the bottle once the first weapons were used. NATO was simply incapable of stopping a concerted Soviet drive on the Rhine; every tabletop exercise conducted by the generals responsible for the defense of Europe ended with a NATO nuclear weapon being employed to halt the Soviet Army—and general nuclear war followed.

President Reagan's response was to rebuild an American conventional military, which had been depleted by neglect in the aftermath of the Vietnam War, and to enter into serious nuclear disarmament negotiations with the Soviets, culminating in the elimination of two entire categories of nuclear weapons (short- and intermediate-range nuclear missiles) and meaningful reductions in strategic nuclear weapons. And for a moment, during discussions in Reykjavik, Iceland, Ronald Reagan and his Soviet counterpart, Mikhail Gorbachev, flirted with

Chapter One: *Missiles without a Mission/Object 4202*

the total elimination of nuclear weapons, out of a mutual recognition by both leaders that nuclear war was unwinnable.

The collapse of the Soviet Union led to the emergence of the United States as the world's sole remaining superpower. America did not prove to be a gracious victor in the Cold War, exploiting the weakness of post-Soviet Russia by expanding NATO into the former Soviet satellites of eastern Europe (including the three former Soviet Baltic republics of Lithuania, Latvia and Estonia) and transforming NATO from a defensive alliance to one that conducted offensive operations inside Europe (in Kosovo and Yugoslavia) and out (in Afghanistan and Libya.)

The United States also withdrew from the 1972 anti-ballistic missile treaty, a cornerstone of U.S.-Soviet arms control, leading to the subsequent deployment of American anti-missile capability onto European soil, and a halt to meaningful nuclear arms reduction talks between Russia and the United States (the so-called "New START" treaty negotiated by the Obama administration with Russia is little more than a front for nuclear modernization, with little or no reduction in actual nuclear war-fighting capability on either side).

Moreover, the American nuclear war plan had, void of a Soviet nuclear counter and with little or no respect for the remaining Russian nuclear capability, once again embraced the notion of "limited" or "containable" nuclear conflict, making the once unthinkable an active component of American strategic consideration, including the pre-emptive use of nuclear weapons in a non-nuclear scenario.

The geopolitical situation President-elect Trump will inherit from President Obama is fraught with friction with Russia that, more so today than at any time since the end of the Cold War, has the potential of leading to military conflict. American and Russian forces operate face-to-face in the Baltics. The deteriorating situation in the Ukraine has led to a series of tense confrontations between the U.S. and Russia in the Black Sea region.

In Syria, there is active discussion within the Obama administration about whether to engage in specific military acts—the enforcement of a no-fly zone, the deliberate targeting of Syrian military forces—that would inevitably lead to a shooting war with Russia. And Vice President Biden has publicly endorsed the kind of offensive cyber-attack against Russia (ostensibly in retaliation against unproven allegations of Russian involvement in the hacking of the Democratic National Committee e-mails) that, in and of itself, would constitute an act of war.

Donald Trump was openly mocked during the presidential campaign for his lack of precise knowledge regarding the American triad of nuclear capability—land-based missiles, manned bombers and submarine-launched missiles. In the current environment, however, ignorance may be bliss. Successive American presidential administrations have shown themselves trapped by the allure of nuclear weapons. The triad, born of historical contingencies more than strategic need, is a relic of the Cold War that serves no meaningful purpose today other than to expose the United States, and by extension the rest of the world, to the imminence of nuclear destruction. Viable nuclear deterrence is not dependent on the retention of the triad. And yet the Obama administration has embarked on a trillion-dollar nuclear modernization of the triad, even as it gives lip service to the theory of nuclear disarmament.

President-elect Trump has indicated that he is open to improving relations between Russia and the United States. History has presented him with an opportunity to have a Reagan-like moment, where he could walk the United States away from the precipice of nuclear conflict by entering into meaningful disarmament negotiations with Russia, inclusive of putting the triad on the table (especially land-based missiles,

Chapter One: *Missiles without a Mission/Object 4202*

which serve no viable purpose), and using the savings derived from such to rebuild America's depleted conventional military capability.

The first reduces the potential for devastating nuclear war; the other creates a deterrent to potential miscalculations by any nation doubting American resolve to protect its interests and those of its allies. Both would serve to stabilize and secure America's position in a post-Obama world.

• • •

On October 26, 2016, amid the hubbub of a rancorous American presidential election that dominated the headlines, an event took place in Russia that escaped the attention of those not otherwise involved in monitoring the esoteric world of strategic weapons research and development. This event, a test of a ballistic missile carrying a payload known as "Object 4202," fundamentally changed the landscape of arms control, built as it is on the dual pillars of nuclear deterrence and missile defense.

"Object 4202" is a new kind of weapon, a hypersonic warhead capable of speeds 15 times the speed of sound, and capable of evading any anti-missile system the United States has today or may develop and deploy for decades to come. While the October 26 test used an older RS-26 intercontinental ballistic missile (ICBM) as the launch vehicle, "Object 4202" will ultimately be carried on a newer ICBM, the RS-28.

The RS-28 is itself a wonder of modern technology, capable of flying in excess of five times the speed of sound, altering its trajectory to confuse anti-missile radars, and delivering 15 independently targetable nuclear warheads (each one 10 times as powerful as the bombs the United States dropped on Japan at the end of the Second World War) or three "Object 4202" hypersonic warheads, which destroy their targets through kinetic energy (i.e., through impact).

A nuclear warhead–armed RS-28 would take about 30 minutes to reach the United States from a silo in central Russia; its warheads would be capable of destroying an area about the size of Texas. Armed with the "Object 4202" hypersonic warheads, each of which is capable of destroying an American missile silo, the time would be cut down to 12 minutes or less. The RS-28 ICBM, scheduled to become operational in 2018, assures Russia the ability to annihilate the United States in retaliation for any American first-strike, while providing Russia a silo-killing first-strike capability of its own.

Since the dissolution of the Soviet Union in 1991, Russia has relied on the threat of massive nuclear retaliation as the foundation of its nuclear deterrence strategy, grounded in the notion of "mutually assured destruction," where any nuclear strike by one side would result in a devastating response by the other, thereby reducing the chance of nuclear war.

The glue that held this theory of mutual nuclear suicide together was the 1972 anti-ballistic missile (ABM) treaty, where the Soviet Union and the United States agreed to limitations on the deployment of anti-missile defenses. An effective ABM capability gave a nation the theoretical ability to "win" a nuclear war by launching a debilitating first strike, and then destroying in-flight any retaliatory missiles that survived. Limiting ABM defenses curtailed an arms race by reducing the impetus to develop new weapons capable of breaching an opponent's defenses in an effort to remove the threat of it enabling a first strike.

Effective arms control negotiations must include an appreciation of history, a realistic assessment of the present, and the ability to project into the future.

The ABM treaty provided a foundation of strategic stability, built on the precepts of "mutually assured destruction," that enabled both the United States and the Soviet Union to enter into meaningful arms reduction agreements, including the ground-breaking Intermediate Nuclear Forces Treaty of 1987, and the Strategic Arms Reduction Treaty of 1991. (Ironically, it was President Reagan's insistence in 1986 on continuing the research on the "Star Wars" anti-missile system that precluded the possibility of eliminating nuclear weapons altogether.)

This trend toward nuclear disarmament continued in the decade following the collapse of the Soviet Union, with President Bill Clinton signing a new START II treaty with Russian President Boris Yeltsin in 1993. START II eliminated the deployment of multiple warheads on ICBMs, further stabilizing the strategic balance between the two nations.

But the START II treaty never entered into force. In 2002, George W. Bush's administration withdrew from the ABM Treaty, citing the need to develop defenses against missile launches from so-called "rogue states" like Iraq, Iran, and North Korea. In doing so Bush unhinged the foundation upon which U.S.-Russian strategic arms control was built.

A new arms reduction treaty, signed in 2003, stripped away on-site, inspection-based verification, and did nothing to limit the deployment of ICBMs armed with multiple warheads. While the "New START Treaty" signed by the Obama administration in 2010 brought back limited on-site inspections, there was no prohibition against ICBMs with multiple warheads.

Moreover, the Obama administration continued to develop and deploy anti-missile defenses, both in the United States and in Europe, resurrecting Cold War-era concerns in Russia that the Americans would leverage this new ABM capability to subject Russia to nuclear blackmail, threatening a nuclear strike for which Russia would have no response. Notably, as forewarned above, the subsequent Russian

RS-28 missile system, inclusive of "Object 4202" hypersonic missiles, can trace its origin to the American deployment of ABMs.

These concerns were on display on December 22, 2016, when President Putin delivered a speech that made the recent Russian developments public. "We need to strengthen the military potential of [Russia's] strategic nuclear forces," Putin said, "especially with missile complexes that can reliably penetrate any existing and prospective missile defense systems."

This speech would more than likely have been buried by the American media save for one person—President-elect Donald Trump, who on the same day as Putin's speech tweeted a reply: "The United States must greatly strengthen and expand its nuclear capability until such time as the world comes to its senses regarding nukes."

The president-in-waiting then doubled down on this line of thinking, telling the hosts of MSNBC's "Morning Joe" program the following morning, "Let it be an arms race! We will outmatch them at every pass and outlast them all."

The Russian response was surprisingly muted. Russia, Putin said the following day, was not seeking a new arms race, but only to improve its capabilities in the face of American deployments of anti-missile defenses. Russia was now strong enough to repulse any aggressor, Putin said. "As for Donald Trump, there is nothing new about it; during his election campaign he said the U.S. needs to bolster its nuclear capabilities and its armed forces in general," the Russian president noted.

During the campaign, candidate Trump had been infamously unfamiliar with the basics of American nuclear strategy. At a primary debate, after the moderator underscored the age of America's nuclear arsenal ("The B-52s [a nuclear-capable bomber] are older than I am. The missiles are old. The submarines are aging out"), Trump was asked, "What's your priority among our nuclear triad?" The best the future President could come up with was, "I think...I think, for me, nuclear is just the power, the devastation is very important to me."

There is no doubt that Trump received a more detailed briefing on America's nuclear capability upon being elected. The aging American nuclear arsenal, he would have learned, is a critical national security issue. A new stealth bomber is in development, as is a new class of ballistic-missile submarines. And the Obama administration had initiated a process for producing and deploying a new ground-launched ICBM that would cost the American public $1 trillion over the course of the next decade. This perceived weakness, combined with Putin's public pronouncement of Russian strength, apparently was enough to set the president-elect off on his tweeting and morning-talk-show rant.

A few days shy of his inauguration Trump seemed to have a change of heart. In a wide-ranging interview with British journalists, Trump noted that, "They have sanctions on Russia—let's see if we can make some good deals with Russia." What deal was Trump suggesting? "For one thing, I think nuclear weapons should be way down and reduced very substantially, that's part of it. But Russia's hurting very badly right now because of sanctions, but I think something can happen that a lot of people are going to benefit." (*The Times* of London speculated that the first foreign policy trip President Trump would embark on would be a nuclear disarmament summit with President Putin; a Trump spokesperson rejected this as "false news.")

While Russian president Vladimir Putin, in a January 28, 2017, phone call with President Trump, was warm to the idea of nuclear disarmament talks with a Trump administration, the Russians overall were dismissive of a deal that traded disarmament for the lifting of sanctions. An offer to engage in nuclear arms control talks, Russian Foreign Minister Sergei Lavrov noted, would be furthered by first reviewing the issue of U.S. sanctions against Russia. But there could not be any direct linkage between the two. The Russian Foreign

Minister also noted that the agenda for any such negotiations should include hypersonic weapons, U.S. missile defenses, space weapons and nuclear testing—in short, a broad range of interconnected issues that the new Trump administration appears ill-equipped to handle at this juncture.

Rex Tillerson, the new secretary of state, has been silent on U.S.-Russian nuclear disarmament. And James Mattis, the new secretary of defense and the one Trump cabinet official who has opined publicly about disarmament issues, appears supportive of fielding a new land-based ICBM, thereby closing the door on the possibility of trading those weapons in exchange for similarly deep cuts by Russia. In his testimony before the Senate Armed Services Committee, Mattis noted that these missiles would be "a cost-imposing strategy on an adversary," noting that "any enemy that wants to take us on is going to have to commit two, three, four weapons to make sure they take each one out."

James Mattis would do well to speak to the men and women who operate America's land-based ICBM force today. The Cold War is over, and these missiles no longer stand on the frontline of American defense. If the best reasoning for the continued deployment of land-based ICBMs is that they serve as a sump for a potential enemy attack, then there is no real justification for their existence, now or in the future.

President Trump reportedly told President Putin during their January 28 conversation that the current arms control treaty, up for renegotiation in 2018, was one sided in favor of the Russians. With all due respect to Donald Trump, his American-centric view of the Obama-era arms agreement is moot; the U.S.-Russian arms race is over, and Russia has won.

The RS-28 missile will be operational next year; the new American land-based ICBM won't be operational for another decade. Russia is on the verge of deploying a hypersonic, missile silo-killing

Chapter One: *Missiles without a Mission/Object 4202*

weapon that undermines the secretary of defense's thin justification for a new land-based ICBM. Every missile system Russia deploys, or will deploy, is capable of defeating America's missile defense systems, including what is currently deployed and what is envisioned for the future. And Russia is on the verge of completing the deployment of its own anti-missile shield, one that will seal off its air space to bombers, cruise missiles, and ballistic missiles, negating in totality America's nuclear triad.

There is nonetheless a deal to be made with Russia, but it doesn't involve trading the lifting of sanctions for nuclear arms cuts. President Trump would do well to accept Sergei Lavrov's proposed disarmament agenda and expand it to include a new ABM treaty and a new disarmament treaty that not only reduces the numbers of weapons on both sides, but also would include the elimination of multiple warheads on all missiles, land-based and submarine launched.

Effective arms control negotiations must include an appreciation of history, a realistic assessment of the present, and the ability to project into the future. At this juncture, the Trump administration has not demonstrated the level of competence needed to successfully conclude such a complex negotiation. The first step is to embrace disarmament as a positive goal. While President Trump has shown a limited understanding of the nuclear triad, his recognition that nuclear weapons should be "way down and reduced very substantially" is a step in the right direction.

[This chapter is a combination of two articles: "Missiles without a Mission," originally published in *The Huffington Post*, May 8, 2015, and "The Russians have won the Arms Race," originally published in *The Washington Spectator* on March 20, 2017.]

CHAPTER TWO
Can You Hear Me Now?

From 2002 until 2011, Paul Marcarelli, perhaps better known to American audiences as Verizon's "test guy," made a career starring in television commercials, wandering the width and breadth of the United States, holding a phone to his ear and asking the simple question, "Can you hear me now?" Verizon was, and is, in the communications business in which the ability to send a message is only as good as the corresponding ability to receive it.

On Thursday [March 1, 2018], Vladimir Putin, Russia's much-maligned president, delivered his state of the nation address to the Russian Federal Assembly (the Russian national Legislature, consisting of the State Duma, or lower house, and the Russian Council, or upper house). While the first half of his speech dealt with Russian domestic issues—and any American who has bought into Western media perceptions that Russia is a collapsing state, possessing a failed economy, would do well to read this portion of the speech—it was the second half of the presentation that caused the world to sit up and listen.

In this portion of the speech, Putin outlined developments in Russian strategic military capability. The developments collectively signal the obsolescence of America's strategic nuclear deterrence, both in terms of its present capabilities and—taking into account the $1.2 trillion nuclear weapons modernization program President Trump unveiled earlier this year—anything America might pursue in the decades to come.

Some Western observers have derided Putin's speech as simple posturing, a manic effort to project Russian power and with it, global credibility, where none exists. Such an interpretation would be incorrect. There should be no doubt among American politicians, military leaders and citizens alike. "Every word has a meaning," Putin told his audience. The weapons he referred to are real, and Putin meant every word he said.

"Back in 2000," he said, "the U.S. announced its withdrawal from the Anti-Ballistic Missile Treaty. Russia was categorically against this. We saw the Soviet-U.S. ABM Treaty signed in 1972 as the cornerstone of the international security system. ... Together with the Strategic Arms Reduction Treaty [START], the ABM Treaty not only created an atmosphere of trust but also prevented either party from recklessly using nuclear weapons, which would have endangered humankind. ... We did our best to dissuade the Americans from withdrawing from the treaty. All in vain."

"The U.S. pulled out of the treaty in 2002," Putin observed. "Even after that, we tried to develop constructive dialogue with the Americans. We proposed working together in this area to ease concerns and maintain the atmosphere of trust. At one point, I thought that a compromise was possible, but this was not to be. All our proposals, absolutely all of them, were rejected. And then we said that we would have to improve our modern strike systems to protect our security. In reply, the U.S. said that it is not creating a global BMD [Ballistic Missile Defense] system against Russia, which is free to do as it pleases, and that the U.S. will presume that our actions are not spearheaded against the U.S."

Building on his well-known position, delivered in his 2005 state of the nation address, that "the collapse of the Soviet Union was a major geopolitical disaster of the century" that created "genuine drama" in which "the epidemic of disintegration infected Russia itself," Putin said in his 2018 state of the nation address that "apparently, our partners got the impression that it was impossible in the foreseeable historical perspective for our country to revive its economy, industry, defense industry and armed forces to levels supporting the necessary strategic potential. And if that is the case, there is no point in reckoning with Russia's opinion, it is necessary to further pursue ultimate unilateral military advantage in order to dictate the terms in every sphere in the future. ..."

"We ourselves are to blame," Putin said. "All these years, the entire 15 years since the withdrawal of the United States from the Anti-Ballistic Missile Treaty, we have consistently tried to reengage the American side in serious discussions, in reaching agreements in the sphere of strategic stability." However, Putin observed, the United States "is permitting constant, uncontrolled growth of the number of anti-ballistic missiles, improving their quality, and creating new missile launching areas. If we do not do something, eventually this will result in the complete devaluation of Russia's nuclear potential. Meaning that all of our missiles could simply be intercepted."

Putin pointed out that in 2004, he put the world on notice about Russia's intent to defend itself, telling the press: "As other countries increase the number and quality of their arms and military potential, Russia will also need to ensure it has new generation weapons and technology. ... [T]his is a very significant statement because no country in the world as of now has such arms in their military arsenal."

"Why did we do all this?" Putin asked his audience, referring to his 2004 comments. "Why did we talk about it? As you can see, we made no secret of our plans and spoke openly about them, primarily to encourage our partners to hold talks. No, nobody really wanted to talk to us about the core of the problem, and nobody wanted to listen to us. So listen now. ..."

"To those who in the past 15 years have tried to accelerate an arms race and seek unilateral advantage against Russia, have introduced restrictions and sanctions that are illegal from the standpoint of international law aiming to restrain our nation's development,

Chapter Two: *Can You Hear Me Now?*

including in the military area, I will say this: Everything you have tried to prevent through such a policy has already happened. No one has managed to restrain Russia."

This was a message delivered not just to the Russian Federal Assembly, but to the White House and its temperamental occupant, President Donald Trump, to the halls of Congress, where Russia-baiting has become a full-time occupation, and to the American people, who have been caught up in a wave of anti-Russia hysteria fueled by fantastical claims of a Russian "attack" on American democracy which, when balanced against the potential of thermonuclear annihilation, pales into insignificance. Putin spoke, and one would hope that throughout America the modern-day incarnations of Verizon's Paul Marcarelli are making their way into the homes of every American citizen and the halls of power where those the American people elect to represent them reside, and calling out, "Can you hear me now?"

Based upon the reaction to Putin's speech so far, the answer appears to be "no." This refusal to accept the fact that there exists today a new reality carries with it the potential for catastrophic miscalculation. In Pat Frank's 1959 novel, *Alas, Babylon*, an American Navy fighter aircraft flying over the Mediterranean Sea fires a missile that veers off target, striking an ammunition depot near the Syrian city of Latakia, setting off a massive explosion that the Soviet Union uses as an excuse to initiate a retaliatory nuclear strike against the United States.

It doesn't take a stretch of imagination today to paint a scenario in which American and Russian forces clash over Syria. Indeed, a recent incident—in which Syrian militia forces, supported by Russian private military contractors, advanced toward Syrian oil and gas fields occupied by U.S.-backed Kurdish fighters, only to be attacked by American fighter bombers, resulting in hundreds of casualties, including scores of Russian dead—underscores the fact that such clashes are no longer theoretical.

Russian and American aircraft patrol the same airspace. American and Russian troops face off on the ground below. American forces are charged with implementing a policy that is diametrically opposed to the one being pursued by their Russian counterparts. So far, clashes have been limited to proxies, but it is only a question of when, not if, American and Russian forces engage in force-on-force combat.

Syria is not the only geographical point of friction between the United States and Russia. Both the Baltic States and Ukraine find American and Russian forces facing off against one another. American ships and reconnaissance aircraft probing the waters and airspace off the Baltic coast and in the Black Sea have been aggressively challenged by Russian aircraft, oftentimes flying dangerously close to their American counterparts, prompting then-Secretary of State John Kerry to declare that the U.S. Navy would be justified in shooting down the Russians in "self-defense."

The almost cavalier ease with which the idea of Russian-American combat is floated as a possibility by American decision-makers is born out of a misplaced notion of American military superiority which, while reflecting an accurate estimate of the situation 10 years ago, is no longer the case today. After Russia emerged victorious in its short war with the republic of Georgia in 2008, many shortfalls in communications, organization and training were revealed that underscored the second-class nature of the Russian military when compared with the United States and NATO. Russia undertook a crash program, restructuring its military units, professionalizing its ranks, and investing in top-of-the line equipment, including modern communications. The Russian military that occupied the Crimea in 2014 was orders of magnitude better than the one that fought Georgia six years prior. The

Russian military fighting in Syria today (and facing off against the Americans in the Baltics and Ukraine) is even better.

The United States, in recent years, has transitioned away from almost exclusively training for low-intensity conflict in Iraq and Afghanistan, and is once again preparing to fight large-scale combined arms engagements against "near-peer" forces whose training and/or equipment is inferior to the American military. Comments made by U.S. military officers who have recently deployed to the Baltics make it clear that they believe the superiority of American arms serves as a deterrence to Russian regional ambitions. The reality is, even if Russia were to pursue ill-intent against its eastern European neighbors that manifested in military aggression (and there is no indication that this is the case), the notion of American and NATO ground forces serving as a force in deterrence is not sustainable. In fact, in many categories, such as tactical communications, artillery support and armor employment, the Russians outclass their American counterparts. Recent war games show that Russia would defeat NATO in any conflict in the Baltics.

But the quality of the Russian military is not the point. What is important, at least in the context of a broader discussion on comparative nuclear posture, is that 20 years ago, when Russia was militarily inferior to the United States, the Russian leadership embraced a policy of nuclear "de-escalation," which envisioned the early use of tactical nuclear weapons by Russia to offset the conventional military advantages enjoyed by the United States and NATO. Through this policy, Russia sought to leverage its strong capabilities in tactical nuclear weapons by making the cost of regional engagement too high for any potential opponent. The policy of nuclear de-escalation was born during the time of the Chechen crisis in the late 1990s, when Russia feared the possibility of Western intervention in that conflict. It served as the backbone of Russia's nuclear posture in both 2008 and 2014, when Russia intervened in Georgia and Ukraine, respectively. And it backed up Russia's decision to intervene in Syria in 2015.

This Russian nuclear policy was noted in the 2018 U.S. Nuclear Posture Review, which said that "Russian strategy and doctrine emphasize the potential coercive and military uses of nuclear weapons. It mistakenly assesses that the threat of nuclear escalation or actual first use of nuclear weapons would serve to 'de-escalate' a conflict on terms favorable to Russia. These mistaken perceptions increase the prospect for dangerous miscalculation and escalation."

No truer words could have been written. And yet, the Trump administration seems in no hurry to undertake any actions vis-à-vis Russia that would reduce the possibility of any such miscalculation and escalation. While noting in the 2018 Nuclear Posture Review that "arms control can contribute to U.S., allied, and partner security by helping to manage strategic competition among states," the Trump administration went on to declare that "progress in arms control is not an end in and of itself, and depends on the security environment and the participation of willing partners."

It was as if the entire history of U.S.-Russian arms control referred to by Putin in his state of the nation address never happened.

But it is not just history the Trump administration clouds over. The present and future is likewise shrouded in a cloud of wishful thinking that ignores the progress in Russian strategic capabilities promised by Putin in 2004 and delivered upon in 2018. "The United States," the Nuclear Posture Review states, "remains willing to engage in a prudent arms control agenda. We are prepared to consider arms control opportunities that return parties to predictability and transparency, and remain receptive to future arms control negotiations if conditions permit and the potential outcome improves the security of the United States and its allies and partners."

Chapter Two: *Can You Hear Me Now?*

Noting that "there is no 'one size fits all' for deterrence," the 2018 Nuclear Posture Review states that "the United States will apply a tailored and flexible approach to effectively deter across a spectrum of adversaries, threats, and contexts" in order to "communicate to different potential adversaries that their aggression would carry unacceptable risks and intolerable costs according to their particular calculations of risk and cost."

While not specifically naming Russia, the Trump administration put Moscow on notice that it "must understand that there are no possible benefits from non-nuclear aggression or limited nuclear escalation. … [P]otential adversaries must recognize that across the emerging range of threats and contexts: 1) the United States is able to identify them and hold them accountable for acts of aggression, including new forms of aggression; 2) we will defeat non-nuclear strategic attacks; and, 3) any nuclear escalation will fail to achieve their objectives, and will instead result in unacceptable consequences for them."

The Russian president heard the message the United States was communicating. "We are greatly concerned by certain provisions of the revised nuclear posture review," Putin said, "which expand the opportunities for reducing and reduce the threshold for the use of nuclear arms. Behind closed doors, one may say anything to calm down anyone, but we read what is written. And what is written is that this strategy can be put into action in response to conventional arms attacks and even to a cyber threat."

Putin further noted "that our military doctrine says Russia reserves the right to use nuclear weapons solely in response to a nuclear attack, or an attack with other weapons of mass destruction against the country or its allies, or an act of aggression against us with the use of conventional weapons that threaten the very existence of the state. This all is very clear and specific. As such, I see it is my duty to announce the following. Any use of nuclear weapons against

Russia or its allies, weapons of short, medium or any range at all, will be considered as a nuclear attack on this country. Retaliation will be immediate, with all the attendant consequences."

The wide range of strategic nuclear weapons unveiled by Putin in his state of the nation address have stripped bare the pretense of American nuclear deterrence, in which a potential enemy would be intimidated by the promise of assured nuclear destruction from engaging in conduct that threatened American national security interests. Russia, Putin said, is not, and will not, be intimidated by America's nuclear arsenal. Moreover, Russia, taking a page from former President Ronald Reagan's animus toward the notion of "mutually assured destruction," or MAD, does not plan on engaging in a policy of passive deterrence.

Nine years ago, Russian strategic planners factored nuclear weapons into every facet of their military policy, including those involving non-nuclear scenarios. "We have corrected the conditions for use of nuclear weapons to resist aggression with conventional forces not only in large-scale wars," Nikolai Patrushev, secretary of the Russian National Security Council, noted in 2009, "but also in regional or even a local one." Patrushev later added that Russian nuclear doctrine did "not rule out a nuclear strike targeting a potential aggressor, including a preemptive strike, in situations critical to national security."

There is a real risk that the United States will continue to minimize the true strategic capabilities of Russia and brush off the words of Putin as mere posturing. The anti-Russian rhetoric of American politicians in Congress, fueled by the near panic generated by the ongoing investigation of special counsel Robert Mueller into the purported Russian interference in the American election that led to the defeat of Hillary Clinton, only plays into the hands of those who treat the ongoing face-off between the U.S. and Russia as nothing more than a bluff. Nothing could be further from the truth. "Everything I have said today," Putin stated in his state of the nation address, "is not a bluff—and it is not a bluff, believe me—and to give it a thought and dismiss those who live in the past and are unable to look into the future, to stop rocking the boat we are all in and which is called the Earth."

There was a time when the threat of nuclear annihilation was taken seriously by those who held political office and high military position in the United States. America's first generation of arms control and disarmament specialists were weaned on the premise and promise of mutually assured destruction, and all the horrors that entailed. By signing the Intermediate Nuclear Forces (INF) Treaty in 1987, then-President Reagan and Soviet Premier Mikhail Gorbachev initiated a process of nuclear disarmament that, for the first time in the nuclear era, backed those two countries away from the precipice of thermonuclear conflict. It was only a half-joke when one experienced American weapons inspector, when asked what he could see when peering inside a Soviet missile launch canister, responded, "C-h-i-c-a-g-o."

Another inspector, a former analyst who monitored the impact of Russian re-entry vehicles in the Pacific Ocean from aboard a U.S. Navy intelligence gathering ship, noted with pride while monitoring Soviet "launch-to-destruct" operations involving SS-20 missiles, that she was one of the only people who could claim to have seen the Soviet warheads during both launch and impact and lived to tell about it.

Other inspectors, training to perform radiation detection tests at Soviet missile bases containing nine mobile intercontinental missiles aimed at American targets, conducted their preparations with Barry McGuire's "Eve of Destruction" playing in the background.

This kind of gallows humor could only be invoked by those who had lived under the direct threat of imminent nuclear death and were prepared to wage war under such conditions. These arms control and disarmament experts are a thing of the past, replaced by bureaucrats and technicians for whom nuclear war is a hypothetical outcome of theoretical strategic game modeling, and not an ever-present reality.

There is a reason the Trump administration—and to be frank, those of Presidents Clinton, Bush and Obama before him—have treated nuclear disarmament and arms control so cavalierly. The United States walked away from the ABM Treaty, opening the door for the current crisis in U.S.-Russia relations. The Cold War-era START has expired, and the INF Treaty has been reduced to little more than a politicized foil, in which unsubstantiated claims of Russian noncompliance are bandied about to further demonize Moscow in the eyes of the American public.

The New START, which replaced the original START, is set to expire in 2021, with little or no effort being made to keep it alive or use it as a foundation for new, more meaningful arms control agreements.

The practitioners of what constitutes arms control and disarmament policy in America today, unschooled in the ultimate futility of nuclear conflict, actually believe America can fight, and win, a nuclear war. "If deterrence fails," the 2018 Nuclear Posture Review notes, "the United States will strive to end any conflict at the lowest level of damage possible and on the best achievable terms for the United States, allies, and partners. U.S. nuclear policy for decades has consistently included this objective of limiting damage if deterrence fails.

In Pat Frank's book, *Alas, Babylon*, the United States "wins" its nuclear exchange with the Soviet Union—only to survive as a Third World nation dependent upon Brazil and Argentina for its food supplies. But that book was written in 1959, too long ago to resonate with the policymakers of today.

The same can be said of the 1959 film, "On the Beach," in which Gregory Peck plays the role of a Navy submarine officer condemned

Chapter Two: *Can You Hear Me Now?*

to watch the rest of the world slowly die from radiation sickness following a nuclear war between the United States and the Soviet Union.

Even the 1982 ABC television drama, "The Day After," which helped change Reagan's opinion about nuclear weapons and the Soviet Union, is considered old history and as such irrelevant for today's post-9/11 strategic theorists.

"There is no need to create more threats to the world," Putin said, wrapping up his 2018 state of the nation address. "Instead, let us sit down at the negotiating table and devise together a new and relevant system of international security and sustainable development for human civilization. We have been saying this all along. All these proposals are still valid. Russia is ready for this."

The question is: Is America ready and/or willing to work with Russia in these highly politicized times?

Putin's words are hanging there, much like the urgent query of Paul Marcarelli's Verizon "test guy," asking anyone who would listen, "Can you hear me now?" Let's hope someone in a position of responsibility in Washington, D.C., is listening.

Otherwise, new life will be breathed into the old lyrics of McGuire's song: "If the button is pushed, there's no running away, there'll be no one to save with the world in a grave ... you don't believe we're on the eve of destruction."

[This article was originally published in *TruthDig*, March 2, 2018.]

CHAPTER THREE
Satan's Child

Earlier this month in his State of the Nation address to the Russian legislature, President Vladimir Putin unveiled several new strategic weapons designed to nullify any missile defense shield the United States has deployed, is currently deploying, or will seek to deploy in the next 10 to 15 years.

In the aftermath of Putin's address, the world was left wondering what to make of his brash declarations.

In remarks directly citing Putin's speech, President Trump noted the dangers of an arms race, and then went on to a little boasting himself, saying America "was spending $700 billion a year" to make sure that the United States remained "stronger than any other nation in the world by far."

So was Putin's own foray into post-Cold War superpower gamesmanship merely a bluff? The *New York Times* certainly thought so. A front-page article co-authored by two of the Gray Lady's preeminent national security correspondents, Neil MacFarquhar and David Sanger, emphasized what they called "bluff theory" when citing expert opinion on Putin's speech. One such "independent" analyst, Alexander Golts (notable for his anti-Putin commentary), noted that Putin, in his speech, was describing a totally new generation of weapons. "The question is," Golts asks, "is this true?"

MacFarquhar and Sanger mined social media, pulling up the Facebook commentary of another expert, Douglas Barrie, a senior fellow for military aerospace at the International Institute for Strategic Studies in London, whose analysis on Russian military capabilities runs heavy on skepticism. Barrie noted that the weapons Putin described "could alter the balance of power." However, MacFarquhar

Chapter Three: *Satan's Child*

and Sanger noted, Barrie questioned whether Russia was even close to deploying such systems: "Does reality mean you have an item in the budget saying, 'Develop nuclear propulsion for a missile'? Or does it mean, 'We're going to have one ready to use soon'? I'd certainly want to see more evidence to believe that."

The Doubting Thomases quoted in the *New York Times* were matched in their nonchalance by the senior-most advisors to President Donald Trump on matters of national defense and security, Secretary of Defense James Mattis and CIA Director Mike Pompeo. Calling Putin's announced weapons programs "an arms race with themselves," Mattis declared that Russia "can sink all of that money in," noting that "it does not change my strategic calculation." Pompeo told Fox News that "We are following and tracking all of this closely," and that "Americans should rest assured that we have a very good understanding of the Russian program and how to make sure that Americans continue to be kept safe from threats from Vladimir Putin."

The intellectual stasis displayed by both Mattis and Pompeo is disturbing. These are not so-called "experts" drummed up by the *New York Times* to further the anti-Putin narrative that has become the centerpiece of the *Times's* coverage over the years, but rather serious professionals who hold the security of the United States in their hands. Putin's pronouncements during his State of the Nation address weren't a spur-of-the-moment articulation of fantasy, but rather, as he made quite clear, the byproduct of more than a decade of focused intent to counter the threat posed to Russian national security by America's ballistic missile defense programs. Not only had Russia not masked its intentions in this regard, but it had also gone out of its way to make sure that the United States was aware of what it was doing and why. In 2007, Russia purposely leaked details about the RS-28 "Sarmat" heavy missile that featured prominently in Putin's 2018 State of the

Nation address to the CIA in a futile effort to get the United States to seriously engage in arms control negotiations.

The RS-28 is a direct descendant of the R-36 heavy ballistic missile, better known by its NATO reporting name, the SS-18 "Satan," which over the course of its nearly 45 years in service has been an acknowledged game changer in terms of American-Russian strategic balance. The R-36's large throw-weight (almost 20,000 pounds) allowed it to carry either a single extremely large warhead of 20 megatons or 10 independently targetable warheads of 500 to 750 kilotons each (by way of comparison, the American atomic bombs used to destroy the Japanese cities of Nagasaki and Hiroshima at the end of the Second World War possessed yields of 21 and 15 kilotons, respectively). When the R-36 became operational, it gave the Soviets a genuine first-strike capability, able to eliminate over 60 percent of American missile launch control facilities and missile silos while retaining the capability to launch another 1,000 warheads as a second strike, should the United States choose to retaliate.

From its inception, the United States considered the R-36 the single most destabilizing strategic weapon in the Soviet arsenal and eliminating and/or limiting it became a focal point of American arms control efforts. The START I Treaty saw the number of R-36 missiles deployed reduced from 308 to 154, and the entire R-36 arsenal was scheduled to be eliminated under the terms of the START II Treaty. The decision by the United States to withdraw from the ABM Treaty in 2002, however, resulted in Russia withdrawing from the START II Treaty in response, and as such maintaining its fleet of R-36 missiles. Russia had planned on allowing the R-36 missile to be retired through obsolescence with no intended replacement; this was the intent behind its START II negotiating position.

According to the Russian narrative, the unilateral American withdrawal from the ABM Treaty changed this calculus, prompting

Chapter Three: *Satan's Child*

Russia to embark on an expensive service life extension program to keep the R-36 operationally viable through 2020. Russia, according to Putin, had hoped to re-engage with the United States on meaningful arms control negotiations, but the refusal on the part of the Americans to scale back their plans for ballistic missile defense made such efforts stillborn. The Russian defense industry began researching new ballistic missile technologies that could overcome American missile defenses in 2004; this decision was made in public, Putin claims, in the hope that the United States would recognize the inherent dangers posed by such a system and re-engage on meaningful arms control. One of the new missile technologies that was being explored was a follow-on to the aging R-36, known as the RS-28 "Sarmat."

The RS-28 is far more than a follow-on to the aging R-36 missile—it is, fundamentally, an entirely new weapon the likes of which the United States has never seen. The "Sarmat" retains its impressive throw-weight while reducing its overall weight by nearly 50 percent by using advanced composite materials for the missile airframe and employing a new type of liquid-fuel propulsion system—the PDY-99 "pulse detonation" engine—that hyper-accelerates the RS-28 into orbit, reducing the infrared signature of the launch as well as the time available to American early-warning satellites to detect such a launch.

The RS-28 is designed to either be armed with 10 750-kiloton independently targeted maneuvering warheads, each of which can destroy an American ICBM silo or launch control facility, or between 16 and 24 new hypersonic glide vehicles, each tipped with a 150-kiloton nuclear warhead, and likewise capable of taking out any hardened site on American soil. Either configuration provides Russia with the means to avoid launch detection, evade all missile defense systems, and destroy America's land-based intercontinental ballistic missile (ICBM) nuclear force. In short, with the RS-28, Russia possesses a genuine first-strike capability that nullifies one third of America's nuclear triad.

Contrary to Secretary Mattis's dismissive commentary, the RS-28 does, in fact, fundamentally alter the strategic balance between Russia and the United States. Moreover, Mike Pompeo knows full well that the Russians are not bluffing. Both Mattis and Pompeo had been laboring under the false impression that Russia could not afford to field a follow-on to the R-36 missile, especially considering that that missile had been built in the Ukraine during Soviet times, and as such those capabilities were lost to Russian defense industry. The RS-28, however, is a reality—the Russians simply reconfigured their own indigenous missile production capability and will have at least 50 of the new missiles operational by 2020. It's a reality that America's leadership might want to factor into any future policy toward Moscow.

[This article was originally published in *The American Conservative*, March 22, 2018.]

CHAPTER FOUR
MAD no More

A deadly accident in northern Russia earlier this month [August 2019] caused the U.S. arms control community to stand up and take notice. The Russians claim they were testing "isotopic sources of fuel on a liquid propulsion unit," and that only after the test was completed did the engine explode. There was a spike in radiation levels detected in the city of Severodvinsk, roughly 18 miles away, shortly after the accident. Seven people were killed as a result of the explosion, including at least two who died of acute radiation poisoning. Scores of others were exposed to radioactive materials, and subsequently decontaminated and placed under observation. Within days, the Russians declared that all radiation readings in and around the accident site were at normal levels.

Many Western experts believe that the Russians were testing a nuclear-powered cruise missile, the 9M730 "Burevestnik"—known in the West by its NATO designation, the SSC-X-9 "Skyfall"—and that a miniature nuclear reactor these experts believe was used to power the missile exploded. Other experts, including me, question this conclusion. But a recent report by Roshydromet, the Russian agency responsible for sampling air quality, showed the presence of four distinct isotopes in the atmosphere after the accident that are uniquely sourced to the fission of uranium 235, strongly suggesting that a reactor of some sort was, in fact, involved (mitigating against this conclusion is the fact that no iodine 131 was detected; iodine 131 is the most prevalent isotope produced by the fission of uranium 235, and its absence would be highly unlikely in the event of any reactor explosion).

The bottom line, however, is that no one outside the Russians responsible for the failed test know exactly what system was being tested, why it was being tested, how it was being tested, and why that test failed. The Russian government has refused to provide any details about the test. "When it comes to activities of a military nature," Russian President Vladimir Putin said in a press conference a few days after the accident, "there are certain restrictions on access to information. This is work in the military field, work on promising weapons systems. We are not hiding this," he said, adding, "We must think of our own security."

Others were thinking about their own security as well.

"Something obviously has gone badly wrong here," U.S. national security adviser John Bolton said after the accident. Bolton observed that Russia is seeking to "modernize their nuclear arsenal to build new kinds of delivery vehicles, hypersonic glide vehicles, hypersonic cruise missiles," noting that "dealing with this capability…remains a real challenge for the United States and its allies." The U.S. and Russia are currently discussing the extension of the New START treaty on strategic arms reduction, scheduled to expire in early 2021. "If there is going to be an extension of the New START," U.S. Defense Secretary Mark Esper said, "then we need to make sure that we include all these new weapons that Russia is pursuing."

But this is problematic—the new Russian weapons under development are directly linked to the decision by the George W. Bush administration in 2002 to withdraw from the Anti-Ballistic Missile (ABM) treaty, a 1972 agreement that limited the number and types of ABM weapons the U.S. and then-Soviet Union could deploy, thereby increasing the likelihood that any full-scale missile attack would succeed in reaching its target. By creating the inevitability of mutual nuclear annihilation (a practice referred to as "mutually assured destruction," or MAD), both the U.S. and Soviet strategic nuclear forces had served as a deterrent against one another.

Chapter Four: *MAD no More*

The deployment by the U.S. of modern ABM systems in the aftermath of its withdrawal from the ABM treaty, Russia believes, threatens its strategic nuclear force and thereby nullifies its deterrent potential. From the Russian perspective, only by building a new generation of modern nuclear delivery systems specifically designed to defeat U.S. ABM capability can Russia reassert its strategic nuclear deterrent. "We have repeatedly told our American and European partners who are NATO members we will make the necessary efforts to neutralize the threats posed by the deployment of the U.S. global missile defense system," Putin stated during a 2018 speech. According to him, "Nobody really wanted to talk to us about the core of the problem, and nobody wanted to listen to us." Putin unveiled Russia's new nuclear arsenal—which included the Burevestnik missile—and stared into the camera, declaring, "So, listen to us now!"

Complicating matters further is the notion put forward by Esper that the weapons Putin unveiled in 2018 would require that the New START treaty be modified prior to any extension, impeding what otherwise would simply have been an automatic extension, based upon mutual consent, for a five-year period. The Russians took umbrage over this position.

"If we want to really comprehend the core of the matter," Vladimir Yermakov, Russia's deputy foreign minister for nonproliferation and arms control, told the Russian press earlier this month, "it should be noted that the New START Treaty covers specific categories of strategic arms, including intercontinental ballistic missiles (ICBMs), submarine-launched ballistic missiles (SLBMs), heavy bombers and ICBM and SLBM launchers. The Treaty," Yermakov emphasized, "does not cover any other weapons systems." Regarding the failed test of Aug. 8, Yermakov declared: "This also concerns the relevant research and development projects." Yermakov categorically rejected the proposition put forward by Esper, noting that "the question of hypothetically extending the New START Treaty with certain weapons systems that do not fit into the aforementioned categories is absolutely unacceptable."

Esper's position, Yermakov said, did not take the Russians by surprise. "As of late," Yermakov said, "we have been hearing U.S. officials express doubts more and more often as to whether extending the New START Treaty makes sense. It is hard to perceive this as anything other than a conscious effort to lay the required media groundwork and to invent pretexts for declining to extend the agreement after it expires in February 2021 and to obtain absolute freedom to build up the U.S. nuclear arsenal, even to the detriment of strategic stability and international security."

The Russian position on the extension of the New START treaty, Yermakov said, is that it would "be a reasonable and responsible step, making it possible to prevent a complete breakdown in the area of strategic stability," and "would also provide extra time to consider joint approaches towards new weapons systems that are currently emerging and possible new arms control treaties." But before any extension could be considered, the Russian side insisted that the U.S. resolve an outstanding issue of treaty compliance that centered around 56 Trident SLBM launchers and 41 B-52H bombers that were "converted" from their nuclear mission in a way that does not render them incapable of accomplishing that mission. Such conversions are permitted under the New START treaty "by rendering [the Trident SLBM launchers and B-52H bombers] incapable of employing ICBMs, SLBMs, or nuclear armaments."

For the Trident SLBM launchers, the conversion was done by removing gas generators of the ejecting mechanism from the launch tube and bolting the tube covers shut. The problem, for the Russians, is that this procedure is reversible, meaning that the launcher could still be used to launch SLBMs simply by removing the bolts and replacing the gas generators. Likewise, the B-52H modifications involve the removal of launch equipment from the aircraft. The aircraft still retains a socket that would allow the arming mechanism of a nuclear weapon to be connected to the removed equipment, which means the B-52H could be converted back to its nuclear role simply by reinstalling the equipment. According to Yermakov, "Russian inspectors are unable to verify the results of the re-equipping under the procedure stipulated by the Treaty." From the Russian perspective, the issue of the noncompliant "conversion" of the Trident SLBM launchers and B-52H bombers is of "fundamental significance"; any extension of the New START can only be discussed, the Russians maintain, once the United States "fully return to complying with the spirit and the letter of the treaty."

The foundation upon which U.S.-Russian cooperation regarding New START was constructed is fragile, founded as it was on the unilateral abrogation of the ABM Treaty in 2002, the ongoing compliance issue regarding the conversion of treaty-accountable items under New START, and the precipitous decision on the part of the Trump administration to withdraw from yet another landmark arms control agreement, the Intermediate Nuclear Forces (INF) Treaty, which went into effect Aug. 2. It would be the INF Treaty that would deal the fatal blow to U.S. credibility when it came to arms control.

The U.S. had, since 2014, accused Russia of violating the INF Treaty by testing a ground-launched cruise missile (GLCM) to prohibited ranges. According to the U.S. narrative, Russia took advantage of the existence of two other missile systems, the Kh-101 air-launched cruise missile and the Kalibr sea-launched cruise missile, to try and disguise the development of a new GLCM, the 9M729, which the U.S. claims was flight-tested to ranges prohibited by the INF Treaty. "Russia probably assumed parallel development—tested from the same site—and deployment of other cruise missiles that are not prohibited by the INF Treaty would provide sufficient cover for its

INF violation," then-Director of National Intelligence Dan Coats told Congress in January.

For its part, Russia denied that the 9M729 violated the INF Treaty. From the moment the U.S. first raised its allegations regarding the 9M729, Russia requested that they be backed up with facts that would substantiate the claims; this the U.S. refused to do. Finally, to forestall a precipitous U.S. withdrawal from the INF Treaty, Russia displayed the 9M729 alongside its cousin, the 9M728, a similar GLCM that the U.S. acknowledges complies with the range restrictions of the INF Treaty. The Russian Ministry of Defense invited U.S. and NATO military officers stationed in Moscow to attend this demonstration; none did. The Russians were able to demonstrate convincingly that the 9M728 and 9M729 missiles made use of the same propulsion components—solid-fuel rocket motors, which meant that, all things being equal, both missiles would fly the same distance. But there was a kicker—the 9M729 missile was equipped with an improved guidance and control package, as well as a different warhead which, in their aggregate, weighed significantly more than their counterpart components on the treaty-compliant 9M728 missile. In short, the Russians demonstrated that the 9M729 could not fly further than the treaty-compliant 9M728. The U.S. ignored this demonstration.

At the same time the U.S. was accusing Russia of violating the INF Treaty with the 9M729 missile, Russia was voicing similar concerns about the Mark 41 "Aegis Ashore" vertical launch system that the U.S. had installed in both Poland and Romania as part of its ballistic missile defense shield. The Mark 41 originally was designed for service on naval vessels. In this role, its launcher system could be configured to launch either the SM-6 surface-to-air missile, or the Tomahawk sea-launched cruise missile. From the Russian perspective, the Mark 41, when placed in a ground-launch configuration, became an INF-capable system, since it could launch a GLCM of proscribed range. The U.S. was adamant in its rejection of these claims, noting that the Aegis Ashore systems in Poland and Romania were configured to launch SM-6 surface-to-air missiles only. The Russians, however, insisted that there was no physical way to make this determination, noting that the INF Treaty required that similar systems be denoted with unique visually distinctive features; the U.S. dismissed the Russian position as a "technicality."

On August 18, the U.S. conducted a test launch of a GLCM from a Mark 41 launch cannister that had been bolted to a flat-bed trailer, making it a de facto ground launcher. The GLCM flew to ranges greater than those permitted by the INF Treaty. Technically, the U.S. was not in violation of the INF treaty at the time of the test, because it had expired on August 2, some 16 days prior. But those 16 days hold the key to understanding just how seriously Russia took this test. According to a transcript of a meeting Putin held Friday with members of the Russian Security Council, he declared that by conducting a missile test a mere 16 days after the INF Treaty ended, it was "obvious that it was not improvisation but became the next link in a chain of events that were planned and carried out earlier."

From the Russian perspective, they had been right all along—the U.S. had cheated on the INF Treaty, just as they were cheating on the New START Treaty. With such a dismal track record of noncompliance, it is all but certain that the New START Treaty will not be extended and thus liberated from any vestige of constraint, the U.S. and Russia will embark on a new arms race that threatens all of humanity with the all-too-real possibility of imminent destruction.

[This article was originally published in *TruthDig,* August 29, 2019.]

PART TWO

The INF Treaty

CHAPTER FIVE
Missile Madness

The U.S. has accused Russia of violating the Intermediate-Range Nuclear Forces (INF) Treaty, a landmark agreement signed in 1987 that set the stage for all future arms control treaties between the U.S. and Russia. In doing so, the U.S. has threatened to develop new weapons to match those it claims are now in Russia's possession. These accusations come as the U.S. is deploying anti-missile capabilities in Poland and Romania that Russia finds not only destabilizing but also a violation of the INF Treaty. The resulting diplomatic imbroglio threatens to destabilize Europe and the Middle East and puts U.S. policy objectives at risk without a discernible endgame.

Answering questions at a Brussels news conference earlier this month on alleged Russian violations of the INF Treaty, the U.S. Ambassador to NATO, Kay Bailey Hutchinson, said that "the question was what would you do if this [violation] continues to a point where we know that they are capable of delivering. And at that point we would then be looking at a capability to take out a missile that could hit any of our countries in Europe and hit America in Alaska."

The notion of a pre-emptive U.S. attack against Russia caught the attention of the Foreign Ministry in Moscow, which was quick to condemn the remarks. Hutchinson quickly walked back her comments, noting that she was "not talking about pre-emptively striking Russia," but she added that Russia "needs to return to INF Treaty compliance or we will need to match its capabilities to protect U.S. and NATO interests."

The issue of Russia's violation of the INF Treaty was front and center at a recent meeting of NATO defense ministers. "Make no mistake, the current situation, with Russia in blatant violation of this treaty, is untenable," U.S. Defense Secretary James Mattis said. While distancing himself from Hutchinson's remarks, NATO Secretary-General Jens Stoltenberg added that "all [NATO] allies fully agree that it is extremely important that Russia, in a transparent way, comply with the INF Treaty."

At the heart of this controversy is a new Russian cruise missile, the 9M729. The U.S. says this system possesses a range of 2,500 miles, making it a violation of the INF Treaty, which bans ballistic missiles and ground-launched cruise missiles like the 9M729 with a range of 310 miles–3,420 miles, along with their launchers. Russia has deployed at least two battalions equipped with the 9M729 system, giving it—if the allegations concerning the range of these missiles are true—the ability to deliver precision nuclear attacks throughout Europe.

The U.S. claims that its intelligence on this issue is irrefutable. At a meeting of NATO's Nuclear Planning Group in November 2017, the U.S. briefed its NATO counterparts on the substance of the allegations. But it withheld critical information about how the intelligence had been collected, leading many in the audience to be somewhat skeptical of the claims. Germany, a key NATO ally, found that while the claims were credible, they lacked the kind of final proof needed to find the Russians in noncompliance.

Germany's reticence is critical given that one of the options being discussed between NATO and the U.S. is the development and deployment of an intermediate-range U.S. nuclear missile as a counter to the 9M729. It was this very scenario in the early 1980s—the deployment of U.S. Pershing II missiles and ground-launched cruise missiles in response to the Soviet fielding of advanced SS-20 intermediate-range missiles—that laid the foundation for the signing of the INF Treaty in 1987. But the political uproar over supporting U.S. deployment of nuclear weapons in Europe contributed to the fall of Helmut Schmidt's coalition government in 1982, something no German politician has forgotten as this issue is debated today.

One of the main issues is that the U.S. case against Russia is far from clear-cut. While Russia has been less than forthcoming about the development of the 9M729 system, a stance that contributes to misunderstanding on the part of intelligence agencies watching from afar, it is clear that the 9M729 missile was tested at the same time as long-range versions of a Russian naval cruise missile known as the "Kalibr," creating the potential for misinterpretation of data by both the U.S. and NATO. While American officials insist that this is not the case, the U.S.'s unwillingness to provide specific information about how it reached its conclusion has opened the door to skepticism within NATO about the claimed violation, and outright denial by Russia, citing the lack of any proof that substantiates the allegation.

The aggressive posture taken by the U.S. puts NATO in a bind. The most recent U.S. defense budget authorized the Pentagon to spend $58 billion to develop a new class of ground-based cruise missiles that would have ranges prohibited under the INF Treaty. While research of such capabilities is not proscribed by the treaty, this action still puts the U.S. at odds with NATO, which states that remaining in compliance with the INF Treaty is a core value for its members.

Complicating matters further is the fact that the U.S. and NATO aren't the only parties making claims about potential treaty violations. The ground-based deployment of the U.S. Mk-41 universal missile launcher in Poland and Romania is seen by Russia as representing a direct violation of the INF treaty. This move creates the potential for the U.S. to rapidly deploy nuclear-capable ground-launched cruise missiles into Europe as a counter to the perceived threat from the 9M729 system. But it also creates a missile defense shield that the Russians have declared to be inherently destabilizing.

The SM-3 missile employed by the Mk-41 has a range of 600 miles, allowing targets to be struck throughout European Russia. While such a capability does not directly threaten Russian strategic nuclear missiles, the next generation of SM-3 missiles could allow missiles launched from Poland and Romania to shoot down Russian intercontinental missiles in the boost phase, a capability that would threaten Russia's strategic nuclear deterrence.

A critical element of the Mk-41 system is the TPY-2 radar, which provides early tracking information that increases the capabilities of European-based SM-3 interceptors. In 2012, the U.S. deployed a TPY-2 radar to eastern Turkey, ostensibly to detect ballistic missile launches coming out of the Middle East, and particularly Iran. The 2018 U.S. defense budget has allocated several millions of dollars to upgrading the Turkish-based TPY-2 site, located near the town of Malatya, and known as "Site K."

The Turkish-based TPY-2 radar is critical for the functioning of the Mk-41-based NATO missile defense shield, and as such has become embroiled in recent tensions between Turkey and the U.S. Both Iran and Russia, which maintain cordial relations with Turkey and are cooperating with Ankara on regional issues including Syria and the Kurds, have expressed their discontent with the existence of "Site K." Moreover, the political backlash in the U.S. over Turkey's planned purchase of advanced S-400 surface-to-air missiles from Russia has led to some members of Congress threatening to withhold new F-35 fighter aircraft purchased by Turkey. So, it seems increasingly possible that the TPY-2 radar could become a victim of ongoing U.S.-Turkish tensions, an outcome both Russia and Iran are encouraging.

Washington's posture regarding Russian noncompliance with the INF Treaty is a self-inflicted wound that puts U.S. national security interests at risk, both in Europe and the Middle East. The case against Russia has been far from proven, and in any case, the U.S.

response—to deploy a new generation of nuclear-capable missiles to Europe—represents the kind of destabilizing act that would not be supported by NATO, and that could provoke Russia into hardening its own nuclear posture. Moreover, the U.S. deployment of the Mk-41 ground-based universal launcher in Poland and Romania adds to regional instability in both Europe and the Middle East and also exposes the U.S. to potential political counters by Russia and Iran in Turkey, where continued operation of the U.S. TPY-2 radar site is now at risk.

[This article was originally published in *Energy Intelligence*, October 10, 2018.]

CHAPTER SIX
One Minute to Midnight

Late last month, the Bulletin of the Atomic Scientists unveiled its "Doomsday Clock" for the 26th time since its creation in 1947, declaring that the hands on the clock would remain where they had been at the last setting in 2018. Rachel Bronson, the bulletin's president, described the environment in which the bulletin assesses the threats faced by the world today (which have expanded beyond nuclear to include climate change and cyber) as the "new abnormal," and noted that no one should take comfort from the fact that the hands of the clock have not moved.

"This new abnormal," Bronson wrote in her statement explaining the decision, "is a pernicious and dangerous departure from the time when the United States sought a leadership role in designing and supporting global agreements that advanced a safer and healthier planet. The new abnormal describes a moment in which fact is becoming indistinguishable from fiction, undermining our very abilities to develop and apply solutions to the big problems of our time."

William Perry, former secretary of defense under President Bill Clinton, helped unveil the 2019 iteration of the Doomsday Clock. In his remarks, he highlighted President Donald Trump's declaration to withdraw from the landmark 1987 Intermediate-Range Nuclear Forces (INF) Treaty as an indication of the collapsing relationship between the U.S. and Russia. "When you withdraw from treaties, you are losing this important vehicle of dialogue," Perry observed. "My own judgment is, relative to a year ago, we are slightly worse off."

I agree with Perry—the world is worse off today than it was a year ago. I disagree, however, with his use of the word "slightly" to describe the situation we face, and I dissent from the bulletin's decision

Chapter Six: *One Minute to Midnight*

to stay the hands of the Doomsday Clock. Humanity is sleepwalking toward global annihilation, furthered by a collective amnesia about the threat posed by nuclear weapons, especially in an environment void of meaningful arms control. On February 2, the United States suspended its obligations under the INF Treaty, beginning a 180-day process that, once concluded, will lead to the abandonment of that agreement. Russia soon followed suit. The death of the INF Treaty represents far more than simply the end of an era. It is the end of a process—a mindset—that recognized nuclear weapons for their globe-killing reality and sought their reduction and eventual elimination.

The danger of nuclear weapons has always been at the center of the Doomsday Clock. According to its mission statement, the Bulletin of the Atomic Scientists was founded in 1945 by Manhattan Project scientists who "could not remain aloof to the consequences of their work." Two years later, in 1947, the bulletin unveiled its iconic clock, the hands of which were ominously set to seven minutes before midnight. "The Bulletin's clock," the late Eugene Rabinowitch, one of the bulletin's founding editors, noted, "is not a gauge to register the ups and downs of the international power struggle; it is intended to reflect basic changes in the level of continuous danger in which mankind lives in the nuclear age, and will continue living, until society adjusts its basic attitudes and institutions."

In 1953, the Soviet Union acquired the hydrogen bomb. That act, on the back of the Korean War, caused the bulletin to ruminate about the unrestrained development of nuclear weapons and the lack of any meaningful arms control efforts to hold nuclear proliferation in check, and prompted it to move the hands of the Doomsday Clock to two minutes before midnight.

Since then, the hands of the Doomsday Clock have been moved back and forth on numerous occasions; retreats were due largely to arms control efforts undertaken by the major nuclear powers and advances due to the failures of these efforts to achieve any lasting change. At the height of the Cold War in 1984, with the U.S. and the Soviet Union locked in a massive arms race, the Doomsday Clock's hands were moved to three minutes past midnight; in 1988, in recognition of the INF Treaty, the hands were moved back to six minutes, then further to 10 minutes in 1990, marking the end of the Cold War, and to 17 minutes in 1994, on the occasion of the Strategic Arms Reduction Treaty (START). The common denominator in this retrograde movement (which, in the context of the meaning of "midnight," is a good thing) was the embrace of meaningful arms control and the calming effect it had on relationships between nations.

Within three years, the optimism that prompted the bulletin to move the hands of the Doomsday Clock back began to falter; the failure of the U.S. and Russia to conclude the START 3 treaty and the expansion of NATO moved the hands to 14 minutes in 1994, while the nuclear tests conducted by India and Pakistan in 1998 caused the bulletin to advance a further five minutes, to nine minutes (its largest forward move since 1968, when nuclear tests by France and China produced a similar result). The demise of the Anti-Ballistic Missile (ABM) Treaty in 2002 moved the hands to seven; the failure of the nonproliferation treaty in the context of North Korea and Iran pushed them to five in 2007. The election of President Barack Obama injected rare optimism at the bulletin, which moved the hands of the clock back to six minutes in 2010. But his administration's failure to ratify the Comprehensive Test Ban Treaty in 2014 brought the hands back to five minutes, and the election of Donald Trump caused the hands to be moved to 2.5 minutes. The failure of the U.S. and Russia to return to the arms control negotiating table brought the hands to their current position in 2018—two minutes before midnight.

The demise of the INF Treaty is symptomatic of a larger problem—the collapse of arms control as an institution. Viktor Mizin, one

Chapter Six: *One Minute to Midnight*

of the Soviet negotiators involved in the INF Treaty, made note of this reality, and its consequences. "[Soviet arms control negotiators] got their start with the first negotiations for the partial test-ban treaties [in the 1950s]. These were the people with whom the partial [U.S.-Soviet] detente and the idea of peaceful coexistence began ... [t]his was an entire generation of brilliant diplomats, soldiers, and defense industry specialists. It's no coincidence that most competent people around then were the ones who participated in all these negotiations ... [w]e don't have anyone like them now. Both here and in America, there's been a collapse of institutional memory, and no one remembers what happened at these negotiations, and there's nobody who has the same negotiating skills." Worse, Mizin noted, "We're absolutely failing to raise the next generation."

The INF Treaty grew out of an idea—"double zero"—put forward in 1982 by President Reagan in a speech at his alma mater, Eureka College. The ideas presented in the speech were the brainchild of Richard Perle, the archconservative assistant secretary of defense for global strategic affairs. The crux of the proposition made by Reagan was that the Soviet Union would eliminate the totality of its SS-20 intermediate-range missile force. The SS-20 was a new road-mobile missile armed with three 750-kiloton nuclear warheads, and its deployment in 1976 was seen by the U.S. and NATO as a game-changer. In exchange for the Soviets agreeing to eliminate these weapons, the U.S. would forego the deployment of two missiles—the Pershing II and the Ground Launched Cruise Missile—that were still under development. In short, the U.S. position was that the Soviet Union would get rid of more than 1,400 missiles, while the U.S. got rid of nothing. That proposal, according to Thomas Graham, a senior U.S. arms control official at the time, "was seen as impossible and ridiculous."

Converting the "impossible and ridiculous" into reality was the job of a team of negotiators led by two experienced U.S. diplomats—Paul Nitze and Maynard Glitman. Nitze, best known as the architect of America's Cold War policy of containment of the Soviet Union, was a member of the first Strategic Arms Limitation Treaty (SALT I) delegation, considered the most distinguished negotiating delegation the U.S. has ever fielded. This experience served him well during his tenure as chief INF negotiator. In an effort to break the impasse created by the American "Zero Option" position, Nitze undertook his now famous "walk in the woods" with his Soviet counterpart, Yuliy Kvitinsky, where the two on their own agreed to a disarmament formula that would reduce the threat posed by the INF systems. Reagan was initially supportive of Nitze's proposal but backtracked when Richard Perle vehemently objected. "The trouble with you," Perle told Nitze afterward, "is you are just an inveterate problem solver."

In 1983, the Soviets walked out of the INF talks, frustrated at the lack of progress being made. Three years later, after the ascension of Mikhail Gorbachev as leader of the Soviet Union, the talks resumed, this time led by Glitman, who had been Nitze's deputy during the first round of talks from 1981 to 1983. Glitman proved a steady, sobering presence, and by the end of 1987 had negotiated a treaty that saw the elimination of all U.S. and Soviet INF weapons—a true "Zero Option" (Perle, who opposed the INF Treaty, resigned in protest).

The INF Treaty has gone through its fair share of trials and tribulations. As one of the first U.S. inspectors assigned to monitor the Votkinsk missile plant in the Soviet Union, where SS-20 missiles had been assembled, I was involved in helping turn back the efforts of such conservative lawmakers as Sen. Jesse Helms, who sought to use delays in the implementation of inspection procedures at Votkinsk as an excuse to kill the treaty. That these delays were brought on by

Chapter Six: *One Minute to Midnight*

shortcomings on the American side were of no moment to Helms and his allies. Fortunately, sober minds prevailed, and the inspections were conducted in total conformity with the treaty.

The 2002 decision by the U.S. to withdraw from another foundational arms control agreement—the ABM Treaty—stoked frustration inside Russia over what it viewed as the unbalanced nature of the INF Treaty, which prohibited its possession of intermediate-range missiles while the U.S. expanded NATO and fielded missile defense systems in Europe, and other nations, such as China, India and Pakistan, were allowed to develop INF-capable systems without restriction. Russian President Vladimir Putin gave voice to these concerns in 2007, saying, "We need other international participants to assume the same obligations which have been assumed by the Russian Federation and the U.S."

The next year, U.S. intelligence observed a missile test in Russia that it assessed as a violation of the INF range limitations. Additional tests were observed, which led the Obama administration, in 2014, to report Russia to Congress as being in violation of the INF Treaty. Russia vehemently denied these allegations and demanded that the U.S. provide it with the evidence the allegations were derived from, something the U.S. has refused to do. A series of accusations and counteraccusations followed, culminating in the U.S. identifying the offending missile system—the 9M729—and demanding that Russia come into compliance.

There is a solution to be had—the INF Treaty provides for the existence of the Special Verification Commission (SVC) for the express purpose of resolving disputes that may arise during the life of the treaty. The SVC has been engaged on this issue, but the refusal of the U.S. to back up its claims of noncompliance with evidence, and the repeated denials by Russia that it has violated the INF Treaty, have made diplomacy difficult. The primary problem, however, isn't the technical aspects of any controversy over treaty compliance—as a veteran of several such controversies, I can attest that they can be resolved to mutual satisfaction, provided both parties are committed to the process. The issue today is that the U.S. no longer has in its diplomatic arsenal arms control negotiators of the caliber of Nitze or Glitman. These men have passed, and, as Mizin laments, no effort has been undertaken to groom their successors.

The last serving American expert on arms control, Thomas Countryman, was unceremoniously fired by Trump shortly after he took office. I knew Countryman from when he was the U.S. mission in New York's liaison to the United Nations Special Commission on Iraq. By the time of his firing, Countryman was charged with negotiating, implementing and verifying international arms control agreements. "The world doesn't stop turning just because there is a new U.S. administration," Joseph Cirincione, president of the Ploughshares Fund, observed in the aftermath of Countryman's firing. "There is an entire global arms regime to maintain. Without U.S. leadership, decisions won't get made or will get taken in ways that harm our national security."

The woman appointed to fill Countryman's role as chief arms negotiator, Andrea Thompson, is a 25-year veteran of the Army who specialized in intelligence but had no arms control background. She came to the White House in 2017 from the McChrystal Group Leadership Institute, an advisory organization formed by retired Gen. Stanley McChrystal, for whom Thompson worked in both Iraq and Afghanistan. At the White House, Thompson served as the deputy assistant to the president and national security adviser to the vice president, positions that emphasize political loyalty over subject matter expertise.

During his 2019 State of the Union address, Trump outlined the position he has taken regarding the INF Treaty. "Under my administration," he declared, "we will never apologize for advancing America's

Chapter Six: *One Minute to Midnight*

interests. For example, decades ago the United States entered into a treaty with Russia in which we agreed to limit and reduce our missile capability. While we followed the agreement to the letter, Russia repeatedly violated its terms. It's been going on for many years. That is why I announced that the United States is officially withdrawing from the Intermediate-Range Nuclear Forces Treaty, or INF Treaty. We really have no choice."

There was a choice—meaningful negotiations—but Thompson is no Nitze, and her approach toward arms control negotiations was counterproductive. She met with her Russian counterparts in Geneva in January in a last-ditch effort to save the INF Treaty. "I outlined that to my Russian counterparts on specifically what Russia would need to do in order to return to compliance in a manner the United States could confirm," Thompson said in a press briefing after the meeting. "And at the end of the day, this includes the verifiable destruction of Russia's noncompliant missile system."

The Russians, Thompson noted, "paid lip service to transparency. They offered a briefing and demonstration, a static demonstration, of its noncompliant missile system. They continued to dodge questions. They continued to push false information regarding the missile's capabilities and the testing activity. For example, a demonstration that Russia can't possibly address the fact that they previously tested the missile, again I reiterate, they previously tested this missile to Treaty-prohibited ranges."

The physical inspection of missiles has always been a part of arms control agreements. The Russians did put the 9M729 missile on display after Thompson's briefing, inviting military attaches to inspect it and its launcher. The U.S. refused to attend and pressured its European allies to likewise boycott the demonstration. A videotape of the event backed up the Russian claim that the 9M729 was little more than an improved version of an INF Treaty-compliant missile, the 9M728, making use of the exact same solid fuel motor. While the static display alone would not be enough to mollify U.S. concerns, it would have been a giant step toward reaching a resolution of the U.S. allegations.

But Thompson wasn't looking for a resolution. She was looking for capitulation. "As the undersecretary for arms control and international security and a leader within this administration," she said at her briefing, "for arms control to serve its purpose, violations must have consequences. And as I told Russian counterparts yesterday, Russia faces a choice: It can either have its noncompliant missile system, or it can have the INF Treaty. But it cannot have both."

Foreign Minister Sergei Lavrov has declared that Russia tested the 9M729 missile at the range allowed under the INF Treaty, and that the U.S. has provided no proof of the alleged violation. "Only last fall, [the United States] named two dates when, according to their estimates, tests that violated the INF Treaty took place. We explained to them that the tests had indeed taken place, but the range was allowed by the treaty. We asked them to provide some concrete proof of the range violation, such as satellite pictures or something else, but have not received anything," Lavrov said at a news conference.

That the pending demise of the INF Treaty hasn't sent shockwaves around the world is, in and of itself, disturbing. The casual reaction on the part of Congress and America's NATO allies to what is, in effect, the end of arms control is alarming. It is one thing for Congress and NATO to accept without question the unsustained contention on the part of both the Obama and Trump administrations about Russian INF Treaty violations—European relations with Moscow have been strained since the 2014 annexation of the Crimea, and Russia-bashing has been in vogue in the U.S. since the intelligence community's subsequently disproved allegations of Russian meddling in the 2016 presidential election were published in January 2017.

Chapter Six: *One Minute to Midnight*

But the termination of the INF Treaty is part and parcel of the total unwinding of the last remaining vestiges of U.S.-Russian arms control—the New START treaty, which caps the number and type of strategic nuclear weapons delivery systems that can be deployed by both parties. New START expires in 2021, and the unceremonious approach Thompson has taken toward resolving INF Treaty compliance issues has detrimentally affected any chance of an extension to that treaty being negotiated before it expires. "The environment isn't in a place where I can discuss the New START treaty," Thompson said at her INF press conference. For his part, Lavrov observed, "The entire architecture of arms control, including the New START, including the prospects for further nuclear disarmament and the sustainability of the nonproliferation treaty, is in jeopardy."

The Russians have always feared American intermediate-range missiles based in Europe. The Cuban missile crisis of 1962 was driven in large part by the Russian need to respond to the threat posed by the presence of U.S. Jupiter missiles based in Turkey. And the INF Treaty was signed largely because of Russian concerns over the American Pershing II missile, which could strike Moscow in seven minutes or less after being launched from Germany, eliminating any possibility of Moscow being able to determine whether a notification of missile launch was real or false. Moreover, Russia's nuclear posture—launch on detection (meaning Russia would fire its missiles once a nuclear attack had been verified)—would need to be altered to "launch on warning" or, worse, "pre-emptive nuclear attack." The desire to avoid creating the conditions for a nuclear holocaust drove the Soviet Union to sign the INF Treaty in 1987. "The INF treaty was put there in the first place to stop there being a nuclear strike with very little warning time," British security expert Annie Machon has observed. "And that was a step forward at the time—that it is being torn up now is very worrying."

The U.S. Nuclear Posture Review published by the Trump administration has postulated specific scenarios in which nuclear weapons could be used—including against Russia in Europe. With the INF Treaty gone, and the caps on strategic nuclear weapons soon to be eliminated due to the expected demise of the New START treaty, there is real concern that the U.S. and Russia are about to enter into a nuclear arms race that would rival that of the U.S. and Soviet Union in the 1980s. The difference this time is that neither side has a stable of seasoned arms control experts working on the sidelines to avoid catastrophe. Instead, led by the likes of Andrea Thompson, the U.S. is whistling blithely while sauntering down the path of nuclear destruction.

Thompson would do well to digest the words of Putin during a presentation of the Valdai Discussion Club last October. Confronted with a scenario involving an American nuclear attack, he noted that "the aggressor must know that retribution is inevitable, that it will be destroyed." The Russian president did not mince words when it came to recognizing the consequences of any Russian nuclear retaliation. "We are victims of aggression, as martyrs we will go to heaven," Putin told the audience. "And they will just die."

The Bulletin of the Atomic Scientists is wrong to keep the hands of the Doomsday Clock stuck at two minutes to midnight. The situation is far more grave than its assessed "new abnormal" would suggest. The United States is in the process of creating the conditions for a nuclear war with Russia, and the Russian president is calmly talking about global annihilation if such an event transpires.

The world is on the edge of the nuclear abyss. It's one minute before midnight, and we are acting as if we still have time. We don't.

(This article was originally published in *TruthDig*, February 12, 2019)

CHAPTER SEVEN
The Death of a Treaty

Declaring that "there is a new strategic reality out there," President Donald Trump's hardline national security advisor John Bolton announced during a visit to Moscow earlier this week that the United States would be withdrawing from the 31-year-old Intermediate Nuclear Forces (INF) Treaty. "This was a Cold War bilateral ballistic missile-related treaty," Bolton said, "in a multi-polar ballistic missile world."

"It is the American position that Russia is in violation," Bolton told reporters after a 90-minute meeting with Russian President Vladimir Putin. "Russia's position is that they aren't. So one has to ask how to ask the Russians to come back into compliance with something they don't think they're violating."

Left unsaid by Bolton was the fact that the Russians have been asking the U.S. to provide evidence to substantiate its allegations of Russian noncompliance, something it so far has not done. "The Americans have failed to provide hard facts to substantiate their accusations," a Kremlin spokesperson noted last December after a U.S. delegation was briefed NATO on the allegations. "They just cannot provide them, because such evidence essentially does not exist."

Bolton's declaration mirrored an earlier statement by Trump announcing that "I'm terminating the agreement because [the Russians] violated the agreement." When asked if his comments were meant as a threat to Putin, Trump responded, "It's a threat to whoever you want. And it includes China, and it includes Russia, and it includes anybody else that wants to play that game. You can't do that. You can't play that game on me."

Trump appears to have surrendered to the anti-arms control philosophy of John Bolton, who views such agreements as unduly restricting American power. (Bolton was also behind the 2001 decision by President George W. Bush to withdraw from the 1972 Anti-Ballistic Missile Treaty, an act the Russians viewed as inherently destabilizing.) By involving China, which was not a signatory to the INF Treaty, into the mix, the president appears to be engaging in a crude negotiating gambit designed to shore up a weak case for leaving the 1987 arms control agreement by playing on previous Russian sensitivities about Chinese nuclear capabilities.

In 2007, Putin threatened to withdraw from the INF Treaty because of these reasons. "We are speaking about the plans of a number of neighboring countries developing short- and mid-range missile systems," Dmitry Peskov, Putin's spokesperson, said at the time, citing China, India and Pakistan. "While our two countries [the U.S. and Russia] are bound by the provisions of the INF treaty there will be a certain imbalance in the region."

Although unspoken, both Bolton and Trump appear to be trying to drive a wedge between Russia and China. They're doing so as those two nations are coming together to craft a joint response to what they view as American overreach on trade and international security. While the Russian concerns over Chinese INF capabilities might have held true a decade ago, that doesn't seem to be the case any longer.

"The Chinese missile program is not related to the INF problem," Konstantin Sivkov, a member of the Russian Academy of Missile and Ammunition Sciences, recently observed. "China has always had medium-range missiles, because it did not enter into a bilateral treaty with the United States on medium and shorter-range missiles." America's speculations about Chinese missiles are "just an excuse" to withdraw from the INF Treaty, the Russian arms control expert charged.

Chapter Seven: *The Death of a Treaty*

Moreover, China doesn't seem to be taking the bait. Yang Chengjun, a Chinese missile expert, observed that the U.S. decision to withdraw from the INF Treaty would have a "negative" impact on China's national security, noting that Beijing "would have to push ahead with the modest development of medium-range missiles" in response. These weapons would be fielded to counter any American build-up in the region, and as such would not necessarily be seen by Russia as representing a threat.

Any student of the INF Treaty knows that the issue of Russia's national security posture vis-à-vis China was understood fully when the then-USSR signed on to the agreement. During the negotiations surrounding INF in the 1970s and 1980s, the Soviets had sought to retain an INF capability in Asia as part of its Chinese deterrence posture. Indeed, the Soviet insistence on keeping such a force was one of the main reasons behind the "zero option" put forward by the U.S. in 1982, where a total ban on INF-capable weapons was proposed. The U.S. knew that the total elimination of INF systems was a poison pill that Russia simply would not swallow, thereby dooming future negotiations.

Mikhail Gorbachev turned the tables on the Americans in 1986, when he embraced the "zero option" and called upon the U.S. to enter into an agreement that banned INF-capable weapons. For the Soviet Union, eliminating the threat to its national security posed by American INF weapons based in Europe was far more important than retaining a limited nuclear deterrence option against China.

The deployment of Pershing II missiles to Europe in the fall of 1983 left the Soviet leadership concerned that the U.S. was seeking to acquire a viable nuclear first-strike capability against the Soviet Union. The Soviets increased their intelligence collection efforts against U.S. targets to be able to detect in advance any U.S./NATO first-strike attack, as well as a "launch on detection" plan to counter any such attack.

In November 1983, when the U.S. conducted a full-scale rehearsal for nuclear war in Europe, code-named Able Archer 83, Soviet intelligence interpreted the exercise preparations as the real thing. As a result, Soviet strategic nuclear forces were put on full alert, needing only an order from then-general secretary Yuri Andropov to launch.

The Soviet system had just undergone a stress test of sorts in September 1983, when malfunctioning early warning satellites indicated that the U.S. had launched five Minuteman 3 Intercontinental missiles toward the Soviet Union. Only the actions of the Soviet duty officer, who correctly identified the warning as a false alarm, prevented a possible nuclear retaliatory strike.

A similar false alarm, this time in 1995, underscored the danger of hair-trigger alert status when it comes to nuclear weapons—the launch of a Norwegian research rocket was interpreted by Russian radar technicians as being a solo U.S. nuclear missile intended to disrupt Russian defenses by means of an electromagnetic pulse generated by a nuclear air burst. Russia's president at the time, Boris Yeltsin, ordered the Russian nuclear codes to be prepared for an immediate Russian counterstrike, and was on the verge of ordering the launch when Russian analysts determined the real purpose of the rocket, and the crisis passed.

The Europeans had initially balked at the idea of deploying American INF weapons on their territory, fearful that the weapons would be little more than targets for a Soviet nuclear attack, resulting in the destruction of Europe while the United States remained unharmed. To alleviate European concerns, the U.S. agreed to integrate its INF systems with its overall strategic nuclear deterrence posture, meaning that the employment of INF nuclear weapons would trigger an automatic strategic nuclear response. This approach was designed to increase the deterrence value of the INF weapons, since there would be no "localized" nuclear war. But it also meant that given the reduced flight times associated with European-based INF systems, each side would be on a hair-trigger alert, with little or no margin for error. It was the suicidal nature of this arrangement that had helped propel Gorbachev and President Ronald Reagan to sign the INF Treaty on December 8, 1987.

This history seems to be lost on both Trump and Bolton. Moreover, the recent deployment of the Mk-41 Universal Launch System, also known as Aegis Ashore, in Romania and Poland as part of a NATO ballistic missile shield only increases the danger of inadvertent conflict. Currently configured to fire the SM-3 surface-to-air missile, the Mk-41 is also capable of firing Tomahawk cruise missiles which, if launched in a ground configuration, would represent a violation of the INF Treaty. The U.S. Congress has authorized $58 billion in FY 2018 to fund development of an INF system, the leading candidate for which is a converted Tomahawk.

If the U.S. were ever to make use of the Mk-41 in an anti-missile configuration, the Russians would have seconds to decide if they were being attacked by nuclear-armed cruise missiles. Putin, in a recent speech delivered in Sochi, publicly stated that the Russian nuclear posture operated under the concept of "launch on warning," meaning once a U.S. or NATO missile strike was detected, Russia would immediately respond with the totality of its nuclear arsenal to annihilate the attacking parties. "We would be victims of an aggression and would get to heaven as martyrs," Putin said. Those who attacked Russia would "just die and not even have time to repent."

"We'll have to develop those weapons," Trump noted when he announced his decision to leave the INF Treaty, adding "we have a tremendous amount of money to play with our military." Nuclear deterrence isn't a game—it is, as Putin noted, a matter of life and death, where one split-second miscalculation can destroy entire nations, if not the world. One can only hope that the one-time real estate mogul turned president can figure this out before it is too late; declaring bankruptcy in nuclear conflict is not an option.

The United States has a track record of asking nations to prove a negative when it comes to compliance with arms control agreements, and then holding them to account when they fail to do so. The deficit of integrity over U.S. claims against Iraq regarding weapons of mass destruction and Iran and its nuclear program speaks volumes about how corrupt America's policymaking apparatus has become. Now the United States is making the same mistake again by pulling out of the INF Treaty, which it claims Russia violated.

"A high degree of confidence is required before the United States will publicly charge another party with violation of an international agreement." Acting Deputy Director of the U.S. Arms Control and Disarmament Agency (ACDA) Thomas Graham, Jr. delivered those remarks during testimony before the House Permanent Select Committee on Intelligence in 1994. At that time, the ACDA served as the lead agency regarding arms control compliance. The intelligence community supported ACDA's mission of making firm compliance judgments by providing the necessary intelligence information and analysis.

ACDA was supported in this effort by the CIA's Arms Control Intelligence Staff, or ACIS. ACIS provided intelligence support tailored for the specific compliance monitoring and verification requirements stemming from arms control agreements such as the INF Treaty and the Strategic Arms Reduction Treaty (START). It brought to the process a different skill set and mindset than the work being done by the CIA's Nonproliferation Center, or NPC, whose targets were less structured and far more nebulous and nuanced. It was one thing to assess that nation A was exporting technology capable of supporting nuclear enrichment to nation B; it was far different to determine that Russia had destroyed its silos to the depths mandated by a treaty.

For the former, there was far more latitude in interpreting data used to make assessments. The latter required a level of specificity that was unforgiving and often difficult to achieve.

There was a synergy between ACDA and ACIS that extended throughout the intelligence cycle. ACDA would task ACIS with information and analysis. On more technical issues, ACDA would work directly with more specialized organizations within the intelligence community. ACDA, as the lead arms control agency, was responsible for negotiating arms control agreements that, according to Thomas Graham, "have a level of verifiability that is sufficient to provide an acceptable level of confidence regarding other parties' compliance."

As such, ACDA had to be fully appraised about the capabilities and limitations of U.S. intelligence assets so they could appropriately task them with fulfilling specific compliance verification requirements, as well as understanding the limitations of that intelligence. The synergy that existed between ACDA and ACIS allowed for the building of a robust treaty monitoring capability comprised of technical collection systems that were responsive to the specific tasking requirements of policymakers.

But in 1999, the Clinton administration disbanded ACDA, merging its specific arms control functions into a bureau reporting to the undersecretary of state for arms control and international security affairs. This consolidation resulted in the dilution of the relationship between policymakers and the intelligence community. That relationship was further reduced when, in 2001, the intelligence community undertook a similar consolidation, melding ACIS with NPC to create the Weapons Intelligence, Nonproliferation and Arms Control Center, or WINPAC. One of WINPAC's first "accomplishments" was the Iraq WMD fiasco. That was followed in short order by an unimpressive performance on Iran, marked by the use of forged documents, flawed human sources derived from compromised opposition groups, and erroneous analysis—in short, Iraq without the war.

The mindset for tracking WMD proliferation is, by its very nature, different from that of verifying arms control agreements. The first permits actions based on suspicion, while the second mandates a high degree of certainty. Blending these distinct approaches into a singular bureaucratic structure invited intelligence failure, where uncorroborated suspicions were translated into de facto violations in a manner that had been virtually impossible under the former ACDA-ACIS relationship. This consolidation, more than anything else, represents the genesis of the current INF Treaty imbroglio.

Sometime in 2007 or 2008, intelligence analysts began observing activity indicating that the Russians were developing a new ground-launched ballistic missile. The specific intelligence tip-offs remain classified, but based on what little has been reported, it appeared to include aerial imagery of the Kapustin Yar missile test facility, telemetry collected from various test launches of missiles, and all-source monitoring of Russian weapons acquisition processes. These are the established intelligence tools of the trade—and, as the Iraq and Iran examples have shown, they are susceptible to misinterpretation.

According to the current director of national intelligence, Dan Coats, the intelligence community "assesses Russia has flight-tested, produced, and deployed cruise missiles with a range capability prohibited by the Treaty." Coats named the system in question as the 9M729. He noted that the Novator design bureau was the responsible agency, and that the 9M729 missile closely resembled other cruise missiles Novator was developing at the time.

According to Coats, "Russia conducted the flight test program in a way that appeared purposefully designed to disguise the true nature of their testing activity as well as the capability of the 9M729 missile." Coats makes careful use of estimative language, in particular the terms "assesses" and "appeared," which clearly indicate that the American allegations are not absolute, but rather a matter of analytical supposition. This conclusion is furthered by Coats' concluding statement: "Russia probably assumed parallel development—tested from the same site—and deployment of other cruise missiles that are not prohibited by the INF Treaty would provide sufficient cover for its INF violation."

What is clear from Coats' statement is that Novator was conducting simultaneous tests of multiple similar systems. Open-source information confirms that during the timeframe in question, it was working on upgrading the guidance and control systems of the 3M14 "Kalibr" sea-launched cruise missile—which has a range of well over 2,500 miles, but as a sea-launched system is not covered by the INF Treaty—as well as the 9M729, a ground-launched missile. As such, it is plausible that Russia tested the new guidance and flight control system on the 3M14 missile, and then tested the same system on the 9M729 (guidance systems are not covered by the INF Treaty).

It appears that the 9M729 missile that is being deployed by Russia is likely not capable of ranges that violate the INF Treaty. The Russians have provided a static display of the weapon that showed the propulsion system of the 9M729 to be identical to that of the 9M728 missile, which operates at ranges below the threshold set by the INF. In fact, the larger warhead and increased size of the guidance and flight control systems on the 9M729 result in its range being less than the 9M728. Russia has indicated that it is willing to go further—perhaps removing the missile from its sealed launch canister for a more technical evaluation by U.S. specialists—to reinforce the 9M729's compliance.

The U.S. has refused to participate in such an exercise. Andrea Thompson, the current undersecretary for arms control and international security, met with her Russian counterparts in January 2019 prior to the final decision being made to withdraw from the INF Treaty. "I was there to listen," Thompson noted, "but my objective and the message was clear from the administration that Russia must return to full and verifiable compliance with the INF Treaty." According to Thompson, the only acceptable solution was "the verifiable destruction of Russia's noncompliant missile system."

Thompson's Russian opposite, Sergei Ryabkov, responded by noting, "Clearly, the United States was no longer interested in obtaining our substantive response to their questions. This once again showed us that our efforts at transparency have no impact on the decisions taken by the United States, and that they have taken all their decisions a long time ago and are only waiting for Russia to plead guilty."

"A high degree of confidence is required before the United States will publicly charge another party with violation of an international agreement." The words of Thomas Graham hang heavy in the air today. There is nothing about America's case against Russia that meets that standard. Instead, the U.S. seems intent on following in the same path as previous intelligence failures in Iraq and Iran. This time, however, the consequences will resonate beyond regional chaos. By killing the INF Treaty based on flawed intelligence, the U.S. risks global annihilation.

[This article was originally published in *The American Conservative*, February 25, 2019.]

CHAPTER EIGHT
The Consequences of Failure

U.S. President Donald Trump had touted the importance of U.S.-Russian nuclear talks during the Helsinki Summit with his Russian counterpart, Vladimir Putin, last July. Given the Trump administration's track record regarding issues of arms control and nonproliferation, where accusations and threats are made as a means of setting the stage for a grand negotiated settlement, the U.S.'s words and actions may be part of a larger strategy designed to pressure Russia to the negotiating table. If this is the case, the gambit does not seem to be working, and in fact appears to have succeeded only in stoking regional tensions in Europe and the Middle East.

The Trump administration's landmark decision to withdraw from the Intermediate Nuclear Forces (INF) Treaty represents more than the end of an aging Cold War disarmament pact. Coming on the heels of decades of neglect of arms control by successive U.S. administrations, President Donald Trump's precipitous act puts the world on a path toward a renewed arms race between nuclear powers, unfettered by even a rudimentary framework of limitations. During the Cold War, all parties wrestled with how to manage the nuclear genie released with the U.S. bombing of Hiroshima and Nagasaki. Today, nuclear weapons are an afterthought in the defense postures of nations possessing them. This relaxed attitude, however, was a product of decades of mutual agreement, codified through treaties that sought to diminish the utility of the one weapon that could destroy civilization. The end of the INF Treaty signals the end of arms control—and of self-restraint in employment of the world's nuclear arsenals.

The INF Treaty cannot be viewed in isolation as a relic of the Cold War. The ground-breaking agreement, signed by U.S. President

Ronald Reagan and Soviet Premier Mikhail Gorbachev in 1987, for the first and only time eliminated an entire class of nuclear-capable delivery systems. It was an outgrowth of decades of negotiations between the U.S., the Soviet Union, and the rest of the world on how to contain the nuclear threat. Bilateral arms control agreements, such as the Anti-Ballistic Missile (ABM) treaty and the Strategic Arms Limitation Treaty (SALT), were built upon broader multilateral treaties that sought to constrain the spread of nuclear weapons and the possibility of their use. The 1962 Cuban Missile Crisis, which saw the Soviet Union deploy intermediate-range nuclear missiles to Cuba as a counter to similar U.S. missiles in Turkey, was a wake-up call for both the U.S. and Russia on the need for boundaries on the deployment of nuclear weapons.

The urgency for negotiated agreements was born—and accepted among the U.S. and the Soviet diplomatic communities—during the Eisenhower and Kennedy administrations, from the mid-1950s through the early 1960s. By the time the U.S. and Soviets sat down to hammer out the terms of the ABM treaty and SALT, each side had experienced national security teams for whom the desirability of arms control agreements was second nature. This mindset did not end the atmosphere of Cold War confrontation, but it did help create willingness on the part of both parties to look beyond geopolitical hotspots in order to prevent regional disagreements from boiling over into global nuclear confrontation.

The INF Treaty came about when one of these geopolitical hotspots—Europe—evolved in a way that dramatically increased the likelihood of general nuclear war. The Soviet Union was concerned about so-called "forward-based systems," American tactical military aircraft deployed in Europe and Asia. When combined with nuclear-armed aircraft located aboard carriers in the waters off the Soviet coastline, these systems gave the U.S. and its allies the potential to

Chapter Eight: *The Consequences of Failure*

eliminate Soviet intermediate-range nuclear missiles in a first strike, given the immobility of these systems and the relatively long preparation time required for their launch.

The fear was that the U.S. would be able to act more freely regionally if it knew it could eliminate the Soviet intermediate nuclear strike capability, thus reducing Soviet options to only general nuclear war. To circumvent this, the Soviet Union developed and deployed a new intermediate-range missile, the SS-20, which could threaten all of Europe from deep inside Soviet territory.

Deployment of the SS-20 threw Europe into a panic, and in response, the U.S. deployed to Europe its own modern intermediate-range missiles, including the Pershing II. The Pershing II especially concerned the Soviets because, once launched, it could reach Moscow in only five minutes, radically reducing Soviet leaders' respond time in a nuclear crisis. Previous nuclear doctrine, built around the notion of mutually assured destruction, allowed at least 30 minutes for information to be evaluated and diplomatic efforts made to de-escalate.

The reduction of this time to five minutes meant that the entire Soviet doctrine regarding use of nuclear weapons was changed from "launch on detection" to "launch on warning"—meaning the Soviet leadership would no longer wait to ascertain the specific nature of a threat but act immediately once a threat was identified. This in turn prompted a re-evaluation of the U.S. nuclear posture to include the possibility of a pre-emptive nuclear strike. The INF crisis put the world in greater danger of nuclear annihilation than any event since the Cuban Missile Crisis.

Fortunately, both the Soviet Union and the U.S. were able to draw upon experienced arms control negotiation teams who had worked together for more than two decades. The end result was not the INF Treaty alone. The thinking it engendered was expanded into strategic weapons as well— intercontinental ballistic missiles, strategic bombers and submarine-launched ballistic missiles.

The lessons of the INF Treaty, and its overall importance in arms control, were forgotten by successive generations of diplomats who no longer worked under the threat of imminent nuclear destruction. The end of the Cold War brought a mindset that postured the U.S. and its allies as "victors" and relegated Russia to the status of "loser." The imperative to finish the nuclear disarmament process initiated by the INF Treaty no longer resonated. Instead, the U.S. focused on securing nuclear and geopolitical dominance, pushing for the expansion of NATO into nations formerly under the Soviet umbrella. This began during the Clinton administration. President George W. Bush then withdrew from the ABM treaty and allowed the START agreement to be replaced by a less restrictive successor, which, under President Barack Obama, was codified as "New START." It expires in 2021.

The question of Russian compliance with the INF Treaty, which the U.S. drew upon as an excuse for withdrawing, is mooted by the fact that mechanisms existing under the INF Treaty for resolving such disputes were largely ignored by U.S. diplomats, as Secretary of State Mike Pompeo and National Security Adviser John Bolton view disarmament more as an encumbrance than a virtue.

Likewise, the issue of China's INF capability, which was not part of the bilateral U.S.-Russian INF agreement, is a red herring. Chinese INF systems have never represented the destabilizing force that their U.S. and Russian counterparts did. Earlier, this was because NATO and Europe defined the post-war world order, not Asia. The current U.S. angst seems to stem from a new Chinese intermediate-range missile, the DF-26, which can threaten U.S. naval vessels from deep in the Chinese interior. But the U.S. is seeking unilateral disarmament by China, not an arms control treaty based upon reciprocal reductions, a position that is as unrealistic as it is unwarranted.

Chapter Eight: *The Consequences of Failure*

What is at stake today is the aggressive pursuit of U.S. unilateralism in the face of Russian and Chinese unwillingness to accede to unreasonable U.S. demands.

The U.S. decision to withdraw from the INF Treaty not only threatens to set the geopolitical clock back to a time when the nuclear forces of both the U.S. and Russia were on hair-trigger alert. It also creates the likelihood that the New START treaty will lapse in 2021, setting off a renewed arms race. Trump hints at the potential for a new INF Treaty, encompassing Russia, China and others. But this option is dead on arrival: China has refused to consider it, and Russia has indicated it is going to deploy new INF weapons in Europe that make the SS-20 pale in comparison. And this time, there will be no framework of arms control in place to serve as a brake. Instead, the U.S. and Russia will be engaging in an all-out arms race, the consequences of which no one seems to have spent any time pondering.

[This article was originally published in *Energy Intelligence*, February 12, 2019.]

PART THREE

New START

CHAPTER NINE
Hope

This week [early August 2022], in an address to the Tenth Review Conference for the Treaty on the Non-Proliferation of Nuclear Weapons—which had convened at the United Nations Headquarters in New York—U.S. President Joe Biden made a forceful appeal to Russia regarding the need to resume arms control talks. "Today," Biden said, "my Administration is ready to expeditiously negotiate a new arms control framework to replace New START when it expires in 2026." But, he added, "negotiation requires a willing partner operating in good faith. And Russia's brutal and unprovoked aggression in Ukraine has shattered peace in Europe and constitutes an attack on the fundamental tenets of international order. In this context, Russia should demonstrate that it is ready to resume work on nuclear arms control with the United States."

Biden has made arms control a central theme in his dealings with Russia. Indeed, one of his first major acts as president was to sign on to a five-year extension of the Obama-era New START treaty, which had been allowed to languish under the Trump administration. "Extending the New START Treaty," Secretary of State, Antony Blinken, declared in a press release issued at the time, "ensures we have verifiable limits on Russian ICBMs, SLBMs, and heavy bombers until February 5, 2026. The New START Treaty's verification regime," Blinken noted, "enables us to monitor Russian compliance with the treaty and provides us with greater insight into Russia's nuclear posture, including through data exchanges and onsite inspections that allow U.S. inspectors to have eyes on Russian nuclear forces and facilities."

Blinken then added a critical statement. "The United States," he declared, "has assessed the Russian Federation to be in compliance with its New START Treaty obligations every year since the treaty entered into force in 2011."

Unfortunately, Russia cannot say the same about the U.S. Since 2018, Russia has accused the United States of "converting a certain number of Trident II SLBM launchers and B-52H heavy bombers, in the way that the Russian Federation cannot confirm that these strategic arms have been rendered incapable of employing SLBMs or nuclear armaments for heavy bombers." The bottom line is that America accomplished its conversions in a manner which allowed them to be easily reversed, something Russia believed circumvented the intent of New START, which was the permanent reduction of each side's nuclear arsenals.

The U.S. rejected the Russian allegation, noting that New START does not explicitly require the conversions on either the Trident II SLBM launchers or the B-52H bombers to be irreversible. As long as the treaty was in force, the U.S. contended, Russia could use its inspection provisions to verify that the goal of "rendering incapable" was still in place. The Russians, with reason, believe that the U.S. position violated both the spirit and intent of treaty, a position which carried over into the extension of New START.

But Russia's problems with America's compliance are just one of the issues when it comes to judging whether to trust Washington's good faith on arms control overall. The U.S. has walked away from three foundational treaties in the past two decades – the anti-ballistic missile (ABM) treaty in 2002, the Intermediate-Range Nuclear Forces (INF) treaty in 2019, and the Open Skies Treaty in 2020. Likewise, America's intransigence over fairly adapting the Conventional Forces in Europe (CFE) treaty to reflect post-Cold War realities led to its demise. New START is the last man standing when it comes to arms control accords between Russia and the U.S.

Chapter Nine: *Hope*

Biden tried to further strategic arms control with Russia, discussing the matter with President Vladimir Putin during their Geneva Summit in June 2021. The two leaders agreed to pursue "an integrated bilateral Strategic Stability Dialogue" that would "seek to lay the groundwork for future arms control and risk reduction measures." Indeed, two such meetings were on July 28 and September 30, 2021. Following the conclusion of the second round of talks, the negotiators agreed to "form two interagency expert working groups" covering the "Principles and Objectives for Future Arms Control" and the "Capabilities and Actions with Strategic Effects."

But then came the crisis in Ukraine, and the talks gave way to the issue of security guarantees demanded by Russia in the face of NATO expansion, which threatened to bring Ukraine into the fold of the trans-Atlantic military bloc. In direct talks with the U.S., NATO and the Organization for Security and Co-operation in Europe (OSCE) in January 2022, Russia was repeatedly rebuffed in its efforts to negotiate a new European security framework that considered its national security interests, setting in motion the conditions that resulted in Russia initiating its Special Military Operation in Ukraine, prompting President Biden to terminate the strategic stability dialogue, an action which essentially froze U.S.-Russian relations, at least in the arms control field.

Biden's announcement on restarting talks with Moscow took the Russian foreign minister, Sergei Lavrov, by surprise. "No requests on reopening this negotiating process have been made," Lavrov announced during a press conference in Myanmar, adding that the West "has developed a habit of making announcements on the microphone and then forgetting about them."

Regardless of the lack of any prior notice on the part of the U.S., Russia announced that it was ready to engage in arms control talks at any time, the sooner the better. Kremlin spokesperson, Dmitry Peskov, during a conference call with the media, declared that "Moscow has repeatedly spoken about the necessity to start such talks as soon as possible as there is little time left." If the New START treaty expired without a replacement, Peskov said, "it will negatively impact global security and stability, primarily in the area of arms control." For this reason, Peskov noted, "We [Russia] have called for an early launch of talks, but until that moment it has been the U.S. that has shown no interest in substantive contacts on the issue."

Peskov further emphasized that negotiations on a new arms control pact can only be held "on the basis of mutual respect and taking into account mutual concerns."

Washington's push for talks with Moscow, however, appear to be little more than an effort to get Russia to negotiate away the advantage in strategic nuclear weapons delivery systems that it has accrued in recent years through the development of weapons such as the Sarmat heavy intercontinental ballistic missile (ICBM) and the Avangard hypersonic re-entry vehicle. In this way, the U.S. would have Russia walk away from new systems which cost billions of dollars to develop and field, while the U.S. would only be called upon to give up a handful which have not yet been fully tested and deployed (the U.S. is poised to spend hundreds of billions of dollars in the coming years to replace the Minuteman III ICBM, B-2 bomber, and Ohio-class submarine with a new missile [the "Sentinel"], a new bomber [the B-21], and a new submarine [the "Columbia" class]. The high cost of these new weapons is likely to become an issue in a tightening economic environment, which may explain Biden's push for fresh negotiations.

The current U.S. approach to arms control negotiations appears to be one-sided in nature, premised on sacrificing existing Russian capacity for future American systems which are currently under development. In addition to this, the U.S. has a poor track record when it comes to either treaty compliance (the ongoing controversy over New

Chapter Nine: *Hope*

START verification of Trident and B-52 conversions comes to mind), or treaty adherence (the U.S. withdrawals from the ABM treaty, the INF treaty, and the Open Skies Treaty serve as an historical precedent).

The U.S. approach ignores the fundamental approach taken by Russia when it comes to arms control—that any such negotiations must take place as part of a comprehensive restructuring of existing security frameworks that fully integrate Moscow's legitimate national security concerns. This includes issues pertaining to missile defense (including the two U.S. facilities in Poland and Romania), intermediate-range nuclear forces (a ban on the deployment of such systems on European soil), and non-strategic nuclear weapons (the U.S. stockpile of B-61 bombs currently stored in Europe, and releasable to non-nuclear NATO members during any potential conflict.)

The White House has flipped the script when it comes to advancing the cause of arms control. Former U.S. President Ronald Reagan appropriated a Russian saying—"Trust but Verify"—when discussing his approach to implementing the groundbreaking INF treaty back in 1987. At that time, the "trust" was assumed, and the focus was on constructing appropriate verification regimes to ensure treaty compliance.

Today, there is no trust between Russia and the U.S., primarily because of the dismissive manner which the Biden administration has treated the issue of Moscow's concerns over European security that has been inexorably linked to aggressive NATO expansion. But the abysmal track record of the U.S. under existing and past arms control agreements must also be considered. Even if Biden were willing to consider Russia's concerns, the question that must be answered for Russia is whether the Americans can be fully trusted as a partner in disarmament.

As things stand today, the answer to this question is, sadly, "No."

[This article was originally published in *Russia Today*, Aug. 6, 2022.]

CHAPTER TEN
Have Your Cake and Eat it Too

The U.S. wants Russia and China to rein in their respective strategic nuclear arsenals while it modernizes its own nuclear defenses at the same time. When it comes to strategic nukes, the U.S. can't have its cake and eat it too.

The U.S. Senate recently passed the 2021 National Defense Authorization Act (NDAA), allocating some $1.5 billion for research and development of a new generation of intercontinental ballistic missiles (ICBM) known as the Ground Based Strategic Deterrent (GBSD).

The funding of the GBSD occurred despite pressure to divert some or all of the current allocation to support emergency Covid-19 contingencies. One of the major factors behind the decision was a concerted effort on the part of the U.S. Air Force and the commander of U.S. Strategic Command to convince Congress that a failure to fund the GBSD would be tantamount to unilateral disarmament, given that the current U.S. ICBM force, comprised of Minuteman III missiles, will begin "aging out" as the missiles reach their operational expiration dates.

The proponents of the GBSD, however, have a major policy hurdle before them—namely the desire on the part of President Joe Biden to undertake a review of the current U.S. nuclear posture with a view to breathing new life into strategic arms control negotiations that could potentially reduce the size of the U.S. nuclear arsenal.

Many arms control advocates believe that the logical choice for any significant reduction in the U.S. strategic nuclear arsenal would be to do away with ICBMs altogether, eliminating the need for the GBSD. The supporters of the GBSD believe such a move would put the U.S. in danger by increasing the risk of a nuclear attack by limiting the number of targets any potential nuclear foe would need to strike in an effort to preemptively neutralize the U.S. nuclear deterrent.

There is an urgency in this debate driven by two hard-wired calendar dates. The first is the expiration of the recently extended New START treaty.

While the U.S. and Russia agreed to extend this treaty by five years, the fact is this treaty will expire for good come February 2026, leaving the two nations a scant five years to negotiate a follow-on agreement. The other hard date is in 2030, when the Minuteman III ICBM force will begin aging out.

The current GBSD funding authorization envisions the deployment of a fully operational replacement missile by 2029, but this is contingent upon continued funding at ever-increasing levels in the years to come. If a commitment is made to continue fully funding the GBSD with an eye on operational deployment by 2029, it will handicap U.S. arms control negotiators who will have zero flexibility when it comes to devising a negotiating strategy capable of convincing their Russian, and possibly Chinese, counterparts to agree to meaningful cuts in their respective nuclear arsenals.

Land-based ICBMs have been a critical part of the nuclear triad that has underpinned the U.S. nuclear deterrence posture since the 1960s (the other two components being manned bombers and submarine-launched ballistic missiles, SLBMs.)

Today the U.S. maintains a force of 450 hardened missile silos containing 400 Minuteman III ICBMs scattered across Montana, North Dakota, Colorado, Nebraska and Wyoming. This force has been designed to respond on short notice to any nuclear attack. But its most important characteristic today is its role as a warhead "sponge." Any potential nuclear-armed foe would need to allocate at least two nuclear warheads to each silo to have any chance of destroying the Minuteman

III force. The only nation capable of carrying out such an attack today is Russia, which would have to allocate 900 of its 1,600 deployed warheads to have any chance of taking out the U.S. ICBM leg of the nuclear triad.

Supporters of the current nuclear triad contend that without the land-based ICBM "sponge," any potential foe would only need to focus on attacking five targets in the U.S.—three strategic bomber bases, and two submarine bases. These same experts note that the pressure on the most survivable and lethal component of the triad—the SLBM—will increase as force restructuring limits the number of submarines that are on patrol at any given time, and as new possible technologies emerge that can detect submarines more easily, increasing the chances that some or all of the deployed SLBM-carrying submarines could be preemptively targeted. Only by retaining the land-based ICBM, these experts argue, can the U.S. guarantee a high degree of certainty that any nuclear attack against the U.S. or its allies would result in a massive retaliation that no aggressor could hope to survive.

The Minuteman III missile has been in service for more than 50 years, despite being designed to last ten. It has achieved this level of longevity through a series of service life extension programs (SLEP) which, in their aggregate, have resulted in a missile very different from the one originally deployed, possessing upgraded booster rockets, new avionics and guidance systems, and more modern nuclear warheads. But the current fleet of Minuteman III ICBMs will begin to expire beginning in 2029, when many of the upgraded rocket boosters expire, followed by the guidance systems, which will begin to expire in 2031. If nothing is done to extend the life of the Minuteman III missiles, the arsenal of operational missiles will be reduced to 350 by 2033, and fewer than 100 by 2037.

Proponents of the GBSD argue that the fifty-year lifecycle costs associated with fielding a new ICBM, estimated at $159.2 billion, are

Chapter Ten: *Have Your Cake and Eat it Too*

actually cheaper than the fifty-year lifecycle cost of a new Minuteman III SLEP, with a baseline cost of $160.3 billion. They also point out that the GBSD costs go beyond simply putting a new missile in the ground, but also incorporate silo refurbishment and other ground infrastructure improvements, including a new nuclear command and control system designed to survive in a modern environment where cyber-attacks are a real possibility. The new GBSD also incorporates a modular design that allows for rapid retargeting, and flexibility when it comes to the payload carried, allowing for the introduction of new, improved delivery systems.

The scenario painted by the supporters of the GBSD is based upon an all-or-nothing approach—either spend the money of a new ICBM or lose the ground-based leg of the nuclear triad forever. This logic mitigates both against the loss of ICBMs, and for a newer, more capable missile (the GBSD). But it also ties the hands of arms control negotiators trying to come up with a formula that would result in the reduction of Russian and Chinese nuclear arsenals. By keeping the U.S. nuclear triad intact, and by deploying a new, more capable ICBM in the form of the GBSD, the U.S. would eliminate any incentive on the part of either Russia or China to reduce the size and capability of their respective nuclear arsenals. Indeed, the exact opposite would happen—Russia would continue its current nuclear modernization programs, and China would have every reason to invest in enlarging their own ICBM force.

Moreover, there is virtually no chance that the U.S. would unilaterally disarm its ICBM force by allowing the Minuteman III ICBM to age out without a replacement. The solution to this quandary is managing the U.S. ICBM force in a manner that best retains the potential for viable force retention while keeping the door open for the possibility of elimination through new arms control agreements. In this light, the GBSD is the least favorable option, as its funding cycle calls for the production of some 650 new missiles sustained over the course of fifty years. Once this production level is funded and underway, it will be virtually impossible to stop it from reaching completion.

However, the U.S. could seek to extend the life of the existing Minuteman III ICBM force, and then use arms control negotiations as a way to leverage their continued existence as a means of getting the Russians to agree to meaningful reductions in their own arsenal—the heavy Sarmat ICBM comes to mind.

Similar trade-offs could be negotiated with the Chinese, with a reduction/elimination of the U.S. ICBM arsenal offered up in exchange for China agreeing not to field any new generation ICBMs. These negotiations, if they are to have any chance of success, must be concluded in the next five years—a very short time frame when it comes to arms control negotiations. The flexibility afforded by a Minuteman III SLEP would enable and enhance these negotiations, while an irreversible commitment to fund and deploy the GBSD would guarantee their failure. Seen in this light, there really isn't much of a debate. The key question is who will prevail in the future internal U.S. debate over nuclear force posture—the advocates for a continuation of the nightmare of nuclear deterrence predicated on mutually assured destruction (a self-fulfilling prophecy if there ever was one), or the proponents of meaningful nuclear disarmament through viable and verifiable arms control agreements.

[This article was originally published in *Russia Today*, February 20, 2021.]

CHAPTER ELEVEN
No Start to New START

The U.S. seeks to pressure Russia by threatening to reactivate nuclear capability mothballed under the New START treaty if Moscow refuses to renegotiate. All it will accomplish by this is prove it habitually cheats on arms control.

According to *Politico*, "The Trump administration has asked the military to assess how quickly it could pull nuclear weapons out of storage and load them onto bombers and submarines" when the New START treaty limiting the size of the U.S. and Russian strategic nuclear arsenals expires in February. *Politico* sources its story "to three people familiar with the discussions." According to these sources, the request was made to the U.S. Strategic Command as "part of a strategy to pressure Moscow into renegotiating the New Strategic Arms Reduction Treaty before the U.S. presidential election."

What is curious about this report is that U.S. Strategic Command already knows the answer to the request. To meet the level of warhead reductions mandated under the treaty, the U.S. has decreased the number of warheads carried on the Minuteman III intercontinental ballistic missile (ICBM) from three to one, and on its Trident D-5 submarine-launched ballistic missile (SLBM) from up to 14 to around 5 or 6.

The deactivated warheads were reclassified as either active or inactive. Active warheads are kept fully assembled and subjected to the same level of maintenance and upgrades as their operational counterparts and can be reactivated in accordance with guidelines already established by U.S. Strategic Command. Inactive warheads have been partially disassembled, and their reactivation would take longer than for their active counterparts but is similarly regulated by U.S.

Strategic Command directives. Moreover, the U.S. regularly conducts tests where it reconverts the Minuteman III ICBM to a three-warhead configuration to practice for the very activities suggested in the *Politico* article. The timelines associated with this reconversion are well known to U.S. Strategic Command. It is not publicly known whether the U.S. Navy conducts similar re-conversion flight tests of its Trident D-5 SLBMs.

One aspect of this request that, if it were implemented, would fall outside the existing reactivation guidelines set by U.S. Strategic Command is if the U.S. were to reconvert its fleet of Trident ballistic missile submarines from its current configuration under New START to one where no restrictions applied. This possibility raises some interesting questions about U.S. compliance with New START.

According to Section 1, paragraph 3 in Part Three of the Protocol to the treaty,

"If an ICBM launcher, SLBM launcher, or heavy bomber is converted by rendering it incapable of employing ICBMs, SLBMs, or nuclear armaments, so that the other Party can confirm the results of the conversion, such a converted strategic offensive arm shall cease to be subject to the aggregate numbers provided for in Article II of the Treaty and may be used for purposes not inconsistent with the Treaty."

To meet its obligations under New START, the U.S. converted four SLBM launchers on each of its 14 Trident ballistic missile submarines—a total of 56—to remove them from the permitted number of launchers. This conversion was done by removing the gas generators of the ejecting mechanism from the launch tube and bolting the tube covers shut.

On February 27, 2018, the Russian Foreign Ministry protested the American actions, noting that, in regard to the Trident conversions, they were "converted in such a way that the Russian Federation cannot confirm that these strategic arms have been rendered incapable of employing SLBMs."

The Russians were concerned that the Trident SLBM conversions were not irreversible, as required under the terms of the treaty, and that the 56 launchers listed as having been "rendered incapable of employing SLBMs" should rather have been categorized as "non-deployed launchers" and not excluded from the total aggregate count. To put it bluntly, the Russians were accusing the United States of cheating on the New START Treaty.

If true, the threat made by Marshall Billingslea in his interview with the Russian *Kommersant* paper on September 21 to "reconvert our weapons," if applied to the Trident ballistic missile submarine launch tubes, would not only confirm the Russian suspicions, but certify the U.S. as an untrustworthy negotiating partner in any future arms control negotiations, either with Russia or China.

Washington already has one strike against it in this regard: its contention that the Mk 41 launcher used on the Aegis Ashore anti-ballistic missile system could not be used as a cruise missile launcher, and, as such, did not constitute a violation of the Intermediate-Range Nuclear Forces (INF) Treaty. This was shown to be a lie when, less than a month after the U.S. withdrew from the INF Treaty, it conducted a flight test of a cruise missile fired from the same Mk 41 launcher.

If the *Politico* reporting is accurate, the U.S. military has been ordered to carry out an exercise that is redundant insofar as the data is already known, and which does nothing to further U.S. strategic capabilities. Moreover, if the U.S. plans on increasing its SLBM launch capability by reactivating the 56 SLBM launchers ostensibly rendered inoperable under New START, Marshall Billingslea would be undermining his own stated objective of trying to pressure Russia back to the negotiating table before the November 2020 presidential election.

After all, who in their right mind would be willing to negotiate with a proven cheater?

...

Extending the New START treaty until a new arms control agreement can be negotiated is in the best interest of world peace. President Trump, however, seems ready to sacrifice that security for a few points in pre-election ratings.

There is one thing virtually every arms control expert can agree on: extending the Strategic Arms Reduction Treaty, known as New START, past its February 2021 expiration date is essential for preventing a new nuclear arms race between the U.S. and Russia. As such, it should be done even in the face of widespread disagreement over what a new arms control treaty would look like, and who would participate. Despite having previously discounted the need for such an extension, the Trump administration finds itself less than three weeks out from a contentious national election with the incumbent trailing in the polls and desperate for the opportunity to portray the president as being "presidential."

Having reduced the U.S. negotiating position to a simple "take it or leave it" proposition grounded in a series of demands—mandatory Chinese participation, inclusion of Russian tactical nuclear weapons, and the exclusion of NATO nuclear weapons, to cite but three—that Russia immediately dismissed as non-starters, Trump's Special Representative for Arms Control, Marshall Billingslea, suddenly reversed course, flying to Helsinki to engage in last-minute talks with his Russian counterparts to not only extend New START, but also set the framework for a follow-on arms control treaty. To the surprise and dismay of the Russian negotiation team, on October 6, Billingslea issued a statement to the press applauding "important progress" in the talks, followed by a second declaration on October 13 announcing that the two sides had reached "an agreement in principle" on extending New START and implementing additional arms control measures that would be codified in a "gentleman's agreement."

The new measures sought by Billingslea—which include a freeze on the numbers of non-deployed strategic nuclear warheads held in storage by Russia—are, void of comparable concessions by the U.S., a non-starter. Russia has long indicated that any future arms control agreement must consider missile defense. Indeed, the preamble to New START acknowledges the "interrelationship between strategic offensive arms and strategic defensive arms" and declares that "current strategic defensive arms do not undermine the viability and effectiveness of the strategic offensive arms of the Parties."

Since that time, the U.S. has deployed two controversial Aegis Ashore missile defense installations that can be equipped with an advanced variant of the SM-3 interceptor specifically designed to shoot down intercontinental ballistic missiles (ICBMs). While Russia has not made public the conditions under which it would consider any interim "gentleman's agreement," logic would dictate that such an agreement include missile defense, especially if it were being called on to freeze non-deployed nuclear warheads—the one area in New START where it holds a significant numerical advantage.

Not surprisingly, Billingslea's announcement of an "agreement in principle" was quickly shot down by the Russian foreign ministry, which called the U.S. Special Representative's statement a "delusion" and a "fraud." Russia's Deputy Foreign Minister, Sergei Ryabkov, noted that the U.S. conditions were "unacceptable" and added that it was unlikely that Russia would approve an extension of the New START treaty prior to the U.S. presidential election on November 3.

In the world of arms control negotiations, a one-month delay in the resumption of talks is often a blessing in disguise, as it allows each side to regroup and refine their respective positions. For its part,

Russia had apparently been prepared to incorporate two of its five new types of strategic nuclear delivery systems into the New START framework—a move that would greatly alleviate U.S. concerns about a possible Russian "breakout," even if New START were to be extended. But the unilateralist approach by the U.S. negotiating team, which demanded much from the Russians without giving anything, alienated even the most stoic diplomats on the Russian side. As things stand, there is virtually zero chance that an agreement between the U.S. and Russia could be reached prior to Americans going to the polls on November 3.

Despite having the door slammed in his face by his Russian counterparts, Billingslea continued to portray his negotiations with the Russians in an optimistic light that, at best, represented an unrealistic interpretation of actual events and, at worst, outright fabrication. "We believe that there is an agreement in principle at the highest levels of our two governments," he said in remarks to the Heritage Foundation shortly after the talks in Helsinki ended. "That's why I cut short my trip to Asia and made a beeline for Helsinki when the Russians called and wanted to sit down."

Billingslea placed the blame for any misunderstanding between the U.S. and Russia squarely on the shoulders of the Russian negotiating team, which he alluded to being out of touch with the intentions of President Putin when it came to New START. "I am hopeful that sort of gentleman's agreement—that arrangement we believe has been reached at the highest levels— will ultimately need to percolate down through their system so that my counterpart hopefully will be authorized to negotiate," Billingslea said. "We're ready to strike this deal. We could strike it tomorrow, in fact, but Moscow's going to have to show the political will to do so as well."

In either case, his words, while seemingly directed at his Russian counterparts, were, in fact, intended for domestic political

Chapter Eleven: *No Start to New START*

consumption. The fact is the Trump administration doesn't need to actually have concluded an agreement with Russia prior to November 3 as much as it needs to project to the American electorate—especially those voters who view Trump as a master deal maker—the notion that the president is on the verge of such an agreement. In this way, the U.S. delusion over a non-existent "agreement in principle" is transformed into the illusion of arms control. And that's an act of political deception that might garner Trump the votes he needs come election day, but for which the American public will pay for in spades once New START expires and an arms race the U.S. can't afford becomes a reality.

•••

Less than a week after U.S.-Russian talks on the future of the New START treaty collapsed—amid recriminations from both sides stemming from a misunderstanding, whether deliberate or otherwise, regarding Moscow's position—President Vladimir Putin intervened in a high-profile bid to inject both clarity and a sense of urgency about the future viability of the last remaining arms control agreement between Russia and the U.S.

In a live, public broadcast of a video conference between Putin and the Security Council of the Russian Federation, the president issued instructions that left no doubt as to either his intent or that of his diplomats when it comes to New START. After noting that it had "worked properly" during its history in "performing its fundamental role as a constraint curtailing the arms race and a tool of arms control," Putin instructed Foreign Minister Sergey Lavrov that the Russian position was

> ...to extend the treaty now in effect unconditionally for at least a year in order to have a chance to hold substantive

talks on all the parameters of problems that are regulated by treaties of this kind, lest we leave our countries and all nations of the world with a vested interest in maintaining strategic stability without such a fundamental document as the Strategic Offensive Arms Limitation Treaty (i.e., New START.)

Putin further instructed him to

...formulate our position to the U.S. partners and try to obtain at least some comprehensible reply from them as soon as possible.

Putin's directive came after a presentation by Lavrov on the current situation regarding U.S.-Russian talks on "strategic stability." Far from shutting the door on further negotiations, Lavrov articulated an environment of ongoing dialogue about so-called "new agreements" derived from Russian proposals "in furtherance of the comprehensive approach of strategic stability" presented to the U.S. negotiating team led by U.S. Presidential Advisor for Arms Control Marshall Billingslea.

The American side had put forward its own proposals, presented as "preconditions" for the extension of New START, which, according to Lavrov, "have been formulated both outside the treaty itself and outside [Russia's] frame of reference"—namely, the unconditional five-year extension of New START as set out in the treaty itself.

The U.S. diplomatic offensive regarding a new arms control framework agreement that went beyond the terms and conditions enshrined in the New START treaty appeared to have been triggered by a telephone conversation between Putin and Trump in which

Chapter Eleven: *No Start to New START*

both expressed a desire to see the treaty extended while negotiations regarding a replacement treaty vehicle were underway.

Billingslea appeared to have interpreted this conversation as representing a so-called "gentleman's agreement" to alter the framework mandated by New START to include a freeze on nuclear weapons and other conditions not regulated under the treaty.

While the U.S. stance was rejected by Russian Deputy Foreign Minister Sergei Ryabkov as "delusional," Billingslea, in a video conference with the U.S. conservative think tank the Heritage Foundation, continued to articulate a position suggesting that any problems with the U.S.-Russian negotiation were derived from Ryabkov's failure to comprehend the instructions of the Russian president.

Putin's statement to the Security Council left no doubt as to where Moscow stood on the matter.

Billingslea's mission was always a bridge too far, seeking to compel Russia into accepting what amounted to a new arms control framework that lacked both a legally binding vehicle such as a treaty, and a system of verification. The purpose behind his efforts appeared to be more about domestic American politics, enabling President Trump to claim a major foreign and national security victory on the eve of a contentious national election in which Trump is seeking a second term over a challenge from a Democratic candidate, former vice president Joe Biden, and less about creating a viable, lasting arms control agreement.

Putin's statement put to rest any notion that Trump was going to be able to get the arms control talking point he wanted: that he had personally negotiated an improvement to the Obama-era New START treaty.

The White House immediately rejected the Russian president's offer. The U.S. National Security Council responded via Twitter, apparently written by Billingslea, declaring that a one-year extension of New START was contingent on Russia and the U.S. capping all nuclear warheads during that period, and that "we believed the Russians were willing to accept this proposal when I met with my counterpart in Geneva." Billingslea rejected Putin's offer as "a non-starter."

In the tumultuous world of the Trump White House, where everything appears to be calibrated based on how it will impact Trump on election day, it is not possible to state with any certainty that Billingslea's tweet represents anything approaching the final say on the matter of New START. Putin's proposal made it clear that Russia is open to constructive talks regarding a future arms control agreement that took into consideration U.S. concerns. This, in and of itself, represented a political victory, given that Trump could portray New START as a "failed treaty" he was going to improve.

If he had wanted, Trump could also have accepted the Russian proposal for a one-year unconditional extension of New START and built on Putin's apparent willingness to work toward a new, more expansive arms control agreement as an example of his diplomatic prowess. There are still three weeks before the November 3 election, and anything is possible.

But Putin's words were not just meant for President Trump and those who surround him. Putin expressed his opinion about Biden too, in the context of arms control, in statements made earlier this month.

"Candidate Biden has said openly that he was ready to extend the New START or to sign a new strategic offensive reductions treaty. This is already a very significant element of our potential future cooperation. I would like to repeat what I have said more than once before: we will work with any future president of the United States, the one [to] whom the American people give their vote of confidence," he said.

In this light, Putin's instructions to Lavrov appear to address a larger audience. While Putin declares himself open to a one-year extension of New START at any time during a Trump presidency,

Chapter Eleven: *No Start to New START*

he has also opened the door to a new Biden administration, if the Democrat makes it to the White House. If Biden wins, there will be a brief window between him being sworn in as the 46th president and the expiration of the New START treaty. A one-year extension of New START, void of any preconditions, could be accomplished with, literally, the stroke of a pen.

The thought of Joe Biden getting a major foreign policy victory so early in his administration alone should drive Trump to take up Putin's offer before November 3. But one thing is for certain: Putin doesn't care who he signs an agreement with, just as long as the New START treaty vehicle is preserved while a new treaty is negotiated.

[This chapter is comprised of three articles published in *Russia Today*, on September 29, 2020, October 14, 2020, and October 16, 2020.]

CHAPTER TWELVE
The Death of Arms Control

The U.S. and Russia have stopped all substantive cooperation in the field of arms control, in terms of both implementing existing treaties and negotiating future agreements. There is little likelihood that this cooperation will resume any time soon, leaving both nations locked in a potential nuclear arms race unconstrained by the limits of arms control treaties. The potential for nuclear conflict is greater, as a result, than at any time since the Cuban missile crisis of 1962.

In the early moments of the Biden administration in February 2021, the U.S. was able to agree with Russia a five-year extension to the New START treaty with only two days remaining before it expired. New START, negotiated by the Obama administration in 2010, represents the last remaining strategic arms control agreement in place between the U.S. and Russia. The U.S., during the Trump administration, withdrew from the landmark 1987 Intermediate-Range Nuclear Forces (INF) Treaty in 2019, while the administration of George W. Bush had withdrawn from the Anti-Ballistic Missile (ABM) treaty in 2002.

Speaking to the press in 2021, U.S. Secretary of State Antony Blinken said the Biden administration would seek to use the five years of the New START's renewal to seek an agreement with Russia that further reduced the nuclear arsenals of both sides.

"Especially during times of tension," Blinken noted, "verifiable limits on Russia's intercontinental-range nuclear weapons are vitally important. Extending the New START treaty makes the United States, U.S. allies and partners, and the world safer," Blinken added. "An unconstrained nuclear competition would endanger us all."

Chapter Twelve: *The Death of Arms Control*

Despite the extension, all was not well with the New START agreement. Russia had serious concerns about U.S. compliance regarding the conversion of B-52H heavy bombers and Trident II submarine launchers to make them unable to fire nuclear missiles. According to the Russians (and readily admitted by the U.S.), the conversions were not irreversible, meaning that the U.S. could, in short order, bring the "decommissioned" bombers and launch tubes back into service. The U.S. claims that the treaty text does not define precisely how the decommissioning was to be accomplished, and that the U.S. was in technical compliance.

Adding to these disagreements was the issue of on-site inspections under the treaty. Each side was permitted to conduct up to 18 inspections per year; before being halted in 2020 because of the Covid-19 pandemic, a total of 328 inspections had been carried out by both sides. By the spring of 2021, the U.S. and Russia agreed that inspections could resume. Yet, when the Russians attempted to carry out an inspection in July, the aircraft carrying the inspection team was denied permission to fly through the airspace of European countries due to sanctions banning commercial flights to and from Russia in the aftermath of the Russian invasion of Ukraine. The Russians cancelled the inspection.

Later, in August, the U.S. tried to dispatch its own inspection team to Russia. The Russians denied the team permission to enter, citing issues of reciprocity—if Russian inspectors could not carry out their inspection tasks, then the U.S. would be similarly barred.

The U.S. has periodically raised implementation-related questions and concerns about New START with Moscow through diplomatic channels, according to the State Department, but has determined annually that Russia has complied with its treaty obligations.

Under the terms of the treaty, the U.S. and Russia can convene twice-annual meetings of a body known as the Bilateral Consultative

Commission (BCC), where issues such as the decommissioning methodology or inspections could be discussed at the technical level by experts. The last meeting of the BCC took place in December 2021, prior to Russia's invasion of Ukraine. In the aftermath of rhetoric by both Washington and Moscow regarding the potential employment of tactical nuclear weapons in Ukraine (with the U.S. claiming Russia was preparing for that very possibility, and Russia rejecting such claims while reminding the U.S. and NATO of the conditions under which Russian release of nuclear weapons was possible), U.S. and Russian diplomats began preparations to reconvene the BCC for the purpose of getting inspections back on track and resolving the Russian concerns over decommissioning. When Russia balked at conducting the BCC in Geneva—contending that Switzerland, given its stance in support of Ukraine, could not be deemed a neutral party—the U.S. agreed to change the venue to Cairo, Egypt, with talks scheduled to begin on November 29.

However, at the last second, Russia pulled out of the meeting, citing the ongoing conflict in Ukraine as the reason. Speaking to the press, Russian Deputy Foreign Minister Sergei Ryabkov noted that, "there is, of course, the effect of what is happening in Ukraine and around it. I will not deny it. Arms control and dialogue in this area cannot be immune to what is around it, and the bigger picture—which is rather complex and on the whole disturbing—has affected this."

Russian Foreign Ministry spokeswoman Maria Zakharova further elaborated, declaring that the BCC talks could not be separated from "geopolitical realities," and that the decision to postpone the talks was directly related to "the extremely negative situation in Russian-American relations that was created by Washington and continues to deteriorate steadily."

So far, no date has been set for a rescheduling of the BCC.

Chapter Twelve: *The Death of Arms Control*

In a statement on December 9, U.S. Secretary of State Blinken spoke of the difficulties in the relationship, noting that "there are ... aspects of the relationship where we continue to have some contact, for example on arms control, and we will continue to do that as necessary to try to advance the American national interest."

The reality, however, is that there is no known contact between the U.S. and Russia on arms control. Russia's Foreign Ministry appears to have been taken by surprise by Moscow's decision to walk away from the Cairo BCC, suggesting that the instructions came from the Kremlin itself—and that any possible resolution may have been elevated to the level of Russian President Vladimir Putin and his U.S. counterpart, Joe Biden.

The same day that Blinken issued his December 9 statement, Putin made some comments of his own that hinted at the changing realities governing Russia's approach toward strategic nuclear conflict, and the potential ramifications for the future of U.S.–Russia arms control.

Speaking to reporters, Putin alluded to the recently published U.S. National Security Strategy, and, in particular, the nuclear posture policy contained within. According to Putin, U.S. policy does not exclude the possibility of a "disarming" nuclear first strike, while Russia's nuclear posture policy prohibits such an action. Given this discrepancy in policy positions, Putin said it might be time for Russia to "think about adopting the best practices of our American partners and their ideas for ensuring their security." He added that "if a potential adversary believes it is possible to use the theory of a preventive strike, and we do not, then this still makes us think about those threats that are posed to us."

The New START treaty was negotiated by Russia based on its existing nuclear posture, which dictates force structure and deployment models. If Putin is indeed serious about redefining Russia's nuclear posture, then the existing New START treaty may no longer be a useful tool—Russia would need to develop the technologies and weapon systems suitable for such a task, unconstrained by treaty restrictions.

The New START treaty expires in February 2026. It takes years to negotiate new arms control agreements. As things stand, Russia and the U.S. seem unlikely to be able to replace the New START treaty with a new strategic arms treaty, given the complexities associated with incorporating new weapons systems and emerging technologies into a balanced strategic force matrix acceptable to both parties. The Russians have new weapons systems that are in the process of being deployed, and the U.S. is on the cusp of modernizing its nuclear force. Ideally, such developments would be part of a continuing dialogue about force structure and compliance verification. Such a dialogue is not occurring today, making any future negotiation all the more complicated.

Failure to renew New START would open the door to a world where both the U.S. and Russian strategic arsenals are untethered from the constraints of arms control, while at the same time are being reconfigured for the most destabilizing nuclear postures imaginable—preemptive nuclear first strikes designed to neutralize an opponent's nuclear retaliatory capability.

The risk of nuclear conflict between Russia and the U.S. is greater than any time since the Cuban missile crisis of 1962, and—with relations inflamed by the Ukraine crisis—neither side appears to be in a rush to engage in the processes intended to forestall such an outcome.

•••

In a stunning display of arrogance, ignorance, and hubris, President Trump's new arms control czar threatens to spend America's

Chapter Twelve: *The Death of Arms Control*

adversaries into "oblivion" in any new arms race. But the joke is on him.

Trump's newly appointed Special Presidential Envoy for Arms Control Marshall Billingslea has breathed new life into an historical interpretation that holds the United States won the Cold War with the Soviet Union by escalating an arms race that turned out to be unsustainable for Moscow, bankrupting the Soviet economy and accelerating the collapse of the Soviet Union as a political entity.

In remarks made to the Hudson Institute, a conservative think tank, Billingslea noted that the threat of a new arms race would be enough to bring both China and Russia to the negotiating table for the purpose of crafting a new trilateral arms control treaty that would replace the current bilateral New START treaty, scheduled to expire in February 2021.

"We intend to establish a new arms control regime now, precisely to prevent a full-blown arms race," Billingslea said. If, however, either Russia or China (or both) decided to forego negotiations and continue to pursue new strategic nuclear weapons, then President Trump "has made clear that we have a tried-and-true practice here."

There are numerous factors that mitigate against Billingslea's seeming desire to refight the Cold War. First and foremost, the United States, like the rest of the world, exists in a new post-pandemic economic reality. Whether or not the American people or their elected representatives in Congress are prepared to shoulder the costs of an avoidable arms race with Russia and China while on the cusp of an economic depression is very much a debatable point.

Even if the political will for the kind of open-ended spending extravaganza required to "spend the adversary into oblivion" existed (and with 30-plus million Americans currently out of work, and millions more expected to follow, such thinking rests more in the realm of fantasy than reality), it is virtually impossible for the U.S. today to replicate the conditions that existed back in the 1980s. The current Russian and U.S. defense economies of today are a far cry from those that existed during the Cold War, a fact that bodes well for Russia, and less so for the U.S.

Russian defense industry today is founded on a legacy inherited from Soviet times, when defense industries took precedence over every other aspect of the Soviet economy and attracted the finest scientists and technicians, backed by a virtually unlimited budget. Under former Minister of Defense Dmitry Ustinov, the Soviet ballistic missile production base benefited from a multitude of research and design centers, each connected to its own supporting infrastructure of production facilities responsible for manufacturing diverse components and assembling them into finished products. By 1988, the Soviets had seven different ICBM types deployed. Those were a mix of third-, fourth- and fifth-generation liquid and solid fuel missiles.

While impressive in terms of scope, scale and quality, the Soviet ICBM procurement model was, in the long run, unsustainable. The demands generated by the perestroika reforms initiated by Mikhail Gorbachev beginning in 1985 meant the existing model of multiple design bureaus working in parallel in a virtually competition-free environment had to transition to a missile procurement model driven by cost accounting methods and the limitations imposed by a new era of bilateral strategic arms control agreements.

In the years leading up to the collapse of the Soviet Union, there remained only two missile design bureaus involved in the production of ICBMs. After the fall of the U.S.S.R, one of them—Yuzhnoye—fell under the control of Ukraine.

Today, Russia's JSC Votkinsk Machine Building Plant produces the RS-24 Yars missile, deployed in both a mobile- and silo- based variant, and is developing the RS-26 Rubezh, a modification of the RS-24 capable of deploying the advanced Avangard hypersonic

Chapter Twelve: *The Death of Arms Control*

glide vehicle. Votkinsk also produces the solid-fuel RS-56 Bulava submarine-launched ballistic missile (SLBM), its first foray outside of the world of ICBM development and manufacturing. In a sign of the times, the Makeyev JSC in Miass, which formerly only produced SLBMs, is producing the massive RS-28 Sarmat ICBM, intended to replace the aging R-36 Soviet-era heavy silo-based ICBM.

The new Russian ICBMs are the finest in the world—no nation has anything that can compare, even the United States. They are also among the most cost-effective in the world today. The fact that these missiles are produced in a manufacturing environment plagued by shortages of materials needed to produce critical components is a testament to the resilience of the Russian defense industry, which has literally been forced to both adapt and overcome in the course of the three decades of economically difficult times that have passed since the end of the Soviet Union.

For its part, the U.S. defense industry has been the benefactor of virtually limitless largesse, feeding off a bloated defense budget that has expanded from some $300 billion in 1990 to over $740 billion today. However, over the course of the past 30 years, this money has not been spent on modernizing the U.S. strategic nuclear force. The example of the Minuteman III missiles serves as a point of illustration.

The United States currently deploys a force of 400 Minuteman III silo-based ICBMs. The original Minuteman ICBM was developed at a cost of $17 billion (measured in 2020-equivalent dollars) over the course of five years. The Minuteman III—the version deployed today—is derived from the same 1960s technology and was initially deployed in 1970. Originally designed for a lifetime of some 10 years, the Minuteman III has been subjected to a series of life-extension upgrades that will keep it viable until 2030. After this time, the missile must be replaced.

The U.S. Air Force is currently developing a new silo-based ICBM, known as the Ground Based Strategic Deterrent (GBSD). The missile will be designed to last until 2075, and in addition to incorporating new technologies, will also involve significant upgrades to the related silos and launch control facilities. Current estimates published by the U.S. Air Force for the cost of the GBSD are some $62 billion (by way of comparison, the total Russian military budget is approximately $65 billion).

Even this high cost is disputed by the Department of Defense's Cost Assessment and Program Evaluation (CAPE) office, which projects the actual cost of the GBSD to be between $85 and 100 billion. One of the major reasons for this discrepancy lies in the fact that the United States has not designed a new ICBM since the 1970s, with the MX Peacekeeper. The final contract for the GBSD is expected to be let in September 2020, although as the only bidder, Northrop Grumman, Inc., is expected to be the awardee. This fact alone makes the CAPE estimate seem overly conservative—Northrop Grumman has developed a well-earned reputation in defense industry circles for projects it is involved in coming in over budget and behind schedule. Based upon current examples of contractual cost overruns, the GBSD costs could skyrocket to $200 billion or more, and this number does not incorporate the negative impact on defense procurement resulting from the failure of Congress to pass a defense budget on time, making long-term procurement decisions impossible and further driving up the cost.

The GBSD is but one of a range of modernization programs being planned by the U.S., involving every aspect of its strategic nuclear triad. These programs, which include new manned strategic bombers and new missile-carrying submarines, are expected to cost more than $1.2 trillion over the course of the next 30 years—and these are conservative estimates. Given the spectacular budgetary inefficiencies in

Chapter Twelve: *The Death of Arms Control*

the U.S. defense procurement system today, it is almost certain that any new strategic nuclear weapons system, whether it be an ICBM, SLBM or manned bomber, will cost the U.S. taxpayer far more than originally planned, and more than likely perform far less than originally designed.

Marshall Billingslea can bluster all he wants about spending an adversary into oblivion. The reality is that the U.S. is not prepared, politically or economically, to engage in any new arms race predicated on open-ended budgetary support.

In the Cold War, it was the Soviet Union playing catch-up to U.S. superiority in the field of ballistic missile technology. Today the tables have been turned. Any arms race will find the U.S. operating from a disadvantage right out of the gate, with Russia already fielding the kind of fifth-generation missiles the U.S. has yet to design, let alone produce.

Billingslea is right about one thing—if the U.S. were to engage in an arms race with an adversary where cost was not a limiting factor, the result would, in fact, be oblivion. But the victim would be the U.S., not Russia or China.

[This chapter is comprised of two articles: "The Death of Arms Control," published in *Energy Intelligence*, December 20, 2022, and "U.S. is stuck in Cold War thinking: Plan to spend Russia & China 'into oblivion' in arms race will bankrupt only America," published in *Russia Today*, May 22, 2020.]

PART FOUR

China, North Korea, Iran and Israel

CHAPTER THIRTEEN
Awaken the Dragon

Since the 1960s, China has maintained a no-first-use nuclear policy and pledged never to engage in an arms race but, thanks to the destabilizing impact of U.S. nuclear policy, it has begun an arms race—and it plans on winning.

A quick history lesson: China detonated its first atomic weapon on October 16, 1964. In doing so, it became the fifth country—after the United States, the Soviet Union, the United Kingdom and France—to possess nuclear weapons. Since then, China has developed and deployed a modest arsenal of strategic nuclear weapons delivery systems, with the goal of maintaining a minimum nuclear deterrent against other nuclear-armed powers, with a particular focus on the U.S.

The 2006 Defense White Paper, issued by China's State Council Information Office, provides the most authoritative description of the country's nuclear strategy. China's fundamental goal, the White Paper states, "is to deter other countries from using or threatening to use nuclear weapons against China." This deterrence comes from "principles of counterattack in self-defense" (i.e., "assured retaliation"). China "remains firmly committed to the policy of no first use of nuclear weapons at any time and under any circumstances." Moreover, it "unconditionally undertakes not to use or threaten to use nuclear weapons against non-nuclear-weapon states or nuclear-weapon-free zones."

The White Paper goes on to declare that China "stands for the comprehensive prohibition and complete elimination of nuclear weapons," and that it believes in the "limited development of nuclear weapons" while aiming "at building a lean and effective nuclear force capable of meeting national security needs." In conclusion, the White Paper notes, "China exercises great restraint in developing its nuclear force," and "it has never entered into and will never enter into a nuclear arms race with any other country."

From its inception in 1966, the Chinese People's Liberation Army Rocket Force has relied upon a single missile—the DF-5—as its primary strategic nuclear delivery system. A massive, two-stage liquid-fuel rocket which, depending on what variant one is talking about, can deliver a single warhead (DF-5A), three warheads (DF-5B) or 10 warheads (DF-5C) to targets 12,000 km (7,456 miles) from the point of launch. The DF-5, based in hardened concrete silos, was designed to be able to survive a nuclear attack in sufficient numbers to enable China to deliver a country-killing nuclear counterstrike.

The DF-5, however, had several operational drawbacks which, as the strategic nuclear capabilities of potential adversaries (i.e., the United States) improved, made its survivability in a nuclear conflict more problematic. First and foremost, as a liquid-fuel rocket, it is loaded into its silo with empty fuel tanks. (The fuel and oxidizer used are highly corrosive, and if stored in the missile, would make it unusable in a matter of months.) Before it can be launched, therefore, the DF-5 must be fueled, a process that can take several hours. The Chinese also stored the DF-5 without its warheads. As such, while the missile is being refueled, special teams would be bringing the nuclear warheads from nearby storage shelters and mounting them on the missile body.

The DF-5 is extremely vulnerable during this time, and as the accuracy and time of flight capabilities of U.S. nuclear forces (in particular the Trident D5 system) improved, the Chinese assessed that their DF-5 nuclear deterrent was vulnerable to being taken out by a first strike. Beginning in the 1970s, China began developing solid-fuel rockets for use as mobile intercontinental ballistic missiles (ICBMs).

The first of these, the DF-31, was deployed in 2006, as a road-mobile system. By 2013, the Chinese produced and fielded an improved version, the DF-31A. The DF-31 is armed with a single nuclear warhead. In 2016, China completed testing for a more modern solid-fuel ICBM, the DF-41, which has begun to enter service as a mobile missile. The DF-41 carries 10 independently targeted nuclear warheads.

Between the DF-5, DF-31, and DF-41 missile systems, China was assessed, as of 2019, as possessing around 218 nuclear warheads. (It has an additional 68 nuclear warheads carried on submarines and manned bombers.) But even with this mix of silo-based DF-5s and mobile DF-31/41 missiles, China believed its forces remained vulnerable to a pre-emptive strike by American nuclear and, increasingly, conventional forces. This concern appeared to be magnified in the aftermath of the American withdrawal from the Intermediate-Range Nuclear Forces (INF) treaty in 2019, with an emerging threat of intermediate-range missiles appearing on the periphery of China's borders.

The first sign that China was adapting to this new reality came in the form of significant improvements and additions to its massive Jilantai training area, located near the city of Jilantai in China's Inner Mongolia province. Constructed in 2013, the Jilantai training area was the premier training grounds for the People's Liberation Army Rocket Force, with specialized training constructed for both silo- and mobile-missile operations. Around 2016, however, China began constructing new silos that appeared to be too small to hold the massive DF-5, leading Western analysts to assess that the Chinese were preparing to house their solid-fuel ICBMs, either the DF-31, DF-41 or both, in a silo configuration.

The importance of this distinction is that, while mobility provides for an element of survivability in a classic nuclear exchange scenario, the mobile missiles are vulnerable to loiter weapons, such as armed drones, or precision stand-off weapons, such as the kind of ground-launched cruise missiles being developed by the U.S. in the post-INF treaty era. By placing some of its solid fuel ICBMs in silos, China virtually eliminates the threat from drones and cruise missiles, and because these missiles don't have to be fueled, reduces the vulnerability to U.S. strategic nuclear weapons such as the Trident D5.

The scope and scale of the silo construction led some analysts to conclude that perhaps the Jilantai training area was going to assume a limited operational posture, based upon the number of silos under construction. This assessment was made moot, however, by the discovery of what many analysts believe is a massive missile base, containing 120 silos, under construction near Yumen in Gansu province, and another, containing a potential 110 additional silos, near the city of Hami in Eastern Xinjiang province.

These silos appear to be similar to the new ones seen at the Jilantai training area, leading analysts to assess that the Chinese intend to load them with either the DF-31, DF-41 or both. Many analysts believe that China may opt only to load a few of these silos with missiles, creating the potential for a "shell game" defense that would complicate nuclear targeting by the U.S. But even if only 80 of these silos were loaded with DF-41 ICBMs, China's warhead total would expand considerably, adding up to 800 new warheads to their arsenal.

While China has not publicly released a new nuclear posture statement that supersedes the 2006 White Paper, the construction of new missile silos configured to hold solid-fuel ICBMs possessing multiple warheads changes the nuclear posture options for China. The most likely change is to transition from a pure retaliatory strike capability ("counterattack in self-defense") to a launch-on-warning posture, which means the Chinese missiles would leave their silos when an attack was detected instead of waiting for a nuclear attack to actually occur. Given China's declared nuclear policy, a launch-on-warning posture allows China to retain its no-first-use policy while simultaneously ensuring the survivability of its nuclear forces.

However, if one is an American strategic nuclear planner, one cannot ignore the reality that China is edging close to having a legitimate first-strike capability, especially if it places missiles in every one of the silos under construction. Faced with a potential first-strike capability from both Russia and China, and in light of the growing cooperation between Russia and China on defense issues regarding what both nations view as the growing threat from the United States, the U.S. may be compelled to look at increasing its nuclear arsenal, or dramatically altering its own nuclear force posture and composition, in order to match this emerging threat. This, however, would be a prohibitively expensive proposition.

Which leaves arms control. The Biden administration is currently trying to tie U.S. arms control talks about reducing the strategic nuclear arsenals of the U.S. and Russia to China. Russia has rejected this out of hand, noting that it has nothing to do with the Chinese nuclear arsenal, and therefore the U.S. should be approaching China directly on this matter. U.S.-China nuclear reduction talks, however, are impractical when one compares the relative threat posed by 200-plus Chinese ground-based ICBMs, and the U.S. arsenal of several thousand strategic warheads housed in a nuclear triad consisting of silo-based ICBMs, submarine-launched ballistic missiles and air-delivered nuclear weapons.

The level of reductions in the U.S. arsenal that would make any strategic nuclear forces reduction talks viable for China could not be matched by China, and as such would be politically impossible for the U.S. to agree to. If, however, the Chinese were to complete the two new silo bases and fill them with DF-41s, each of which armed with 10 warheads, then the U.S. and China could negotiate mutually acceptable reductions based on strategic parity. Such negotiations would be complicated by the need to factor in not only Russia, but also the nuclear arsenals of France and the U.K. (as American NATO allies), as well as the nuclear arsenals of lesser powers such as Pakistan, India, Israel and North Korea.

The bottom line, however, is that China appears to have breached its commitment "never to engage in a nuclear arms race of any kind." The facts show that China entered this new phase of nuclear weapons development and deployment as a reaction to developments by potential adversaries (i.e., the U.S.), but let there be no doubt—this is an arms race. The placement of the Chinese silo bases appears, by intent, to be outside the range of anticipated U.S. intermediate-range weapons, such as cruise missiles, meaning that there will be increased pressure placed on the States to field a new generation of silo-based ICBMs to replace the aging Minuteman III missiles, as well as a new generation of submarine-launched missiles and missile-carrying submarines, and a new generation of manned bomber—all in numbers greater than current forecasts call for.

The U.S. cannot afford to enter this kind of arms race with China. Simply put, China has out Ronald Reagan-ed the U.S., flipping the Cold War theory that the U.S. outspent the Soviet Union, bankrupting it, and accelerating its collapse on its head, so that it's the U.S. that's being outspent, bankrupting itself, and pushing itself closer to collapse. Hopefully, the U.S. leadership is wiser than their Soviet counterparts before them. But, if history has shown us anything, the U.S. is addicted to the power it believes it accrues by possessing a large nuclear weapons arsenal, and like any addict, liberating itself from its drug of choice is difficult, if not impossible.

[This article was originally published in *Russia Today* on August 2, 2021.]

CHAPTER FOURTEEN
Escalate to Deescalate

As the U.S. threatens to withdraw from the New START treaty over Chinese non-participation, domestic pressure from inside China builds for a larger strategic nuclear arsenal. Could this be a good thing?

In an op-ed published in Chinese newspaper *Global Times*, its editor-in-chief, Hu Xijin, argued that China should seek to upgrade its strategic nuclear arsenal from its current level of about 200 antiquated weapons to a modernized force comprising more than 1,000 nuclear weapons, including more than 100 modern mobile DF-41 intercontinental ballistic missiles (ICBMs), each armed with 10–12 nuclear warheads, capable of striking the U.S. mainland.

The deployment of DF-41 missiles, when combined with China's new JL-3 submarine-launched ballistic missiles and nuclear-armed H-20 strategic bombers, would give China a capable nuclear triad that rivaled those of the U.S. and Russia.

While Hu Xijin's op-ed received considerable support on Chinese social media, there was some pushback. Zhao Tong, a senior fellow in nuclear policy at the Carnegie-Tsinghua Center for Global Policy based in Beijing, has argued that even in a climate of deteriorating Sino-American relations, any effort on the part of China to build a viable strategic nuclear arsenal on par with that of the U.S. was counterproductive and dangerous.

This point of view has a logic of de-escalation that is inherently attractive, but when viewed in the larger context of global nuclear posture where the U.S. and Russian nuclear disarmament is held hostage by the current non-participation of China in meaningful disarmament talks, any call for China to maintain the nuclear status quo is in itself destabilizing.

The only way to bring China to the table for any meaningful arms control agreement is for it to build up its nuclear arsenal to a level where reciprocal cuts make sense for all involved parties. In short, nuclear symmetry perversely requires that China in effect adopts an "escalate to de-escalate" approach to arms control if disarmament is to have any political viability.

There is a historical precedent for this kind of madness. When the Soviet Union deployed the SS-20 intermediate-range nuclear missile in the late 1970s, it unhinged the strategic nuclear balance in Europe. Both NATO and the U.S. were alarmed and pushed for arms control agreements that eliminated so-called Intermediate Nuclear Forces (INF) from the arsenals of both the U.S. and the Soviet Union. In 1979 the U.S. threatened to deploy advanced Pershing II missiles and Ground-launched Cruise Missiles (GLCMs) into Europe to offset the threat posed by the SS-20 missiles. The problem, however, was that while the SS-20 missile was a reality, the Pershing II/GLCM weapons were still in development stage and had yet to be deployed. From a purely political perspective, there was no incentive for the Soviets to get rid of the SS-20.

Instead, in November 1983, the U.S. and NATO were compelled to go through with the deployment of Pershing II and GLCM missiles to Europe, triggering social and political unrest in the form of massive protests, and placing the U.S.-NATO alliance under considerable stress. Besides, by deploying these new weapons into Europe, the U.S. changed the very calculus of war—the Pershing II, once launched, was less than 10 minutes flight time from Moscow, reducing the time the Soviet command would have to react in a time of crisis regarding the initiation of a general nuclear war.

In the end, the U.S. and the Soviet Union signed the INF Treaty, eliminating the SS-20, Pershing II, GLCM and other nuclear delivery systems, and in doing so heralded a new age of relations between the two sides that helped bring about the end of the Cold War. But the world had to be led to the edge of a nuclear abyss before reason could prevail.

Today the U.S. and Russian strategic nuclear arsenals are capped at 1,550 nuclear delivery systems each by the limits set forth in the New START Treaty. While both sides recognize the desirability of additional reductions, the insistence on the part of the Trump administration that any future arms control agreement on strategic nuclear weapons must include China has thrown a monkey wrench into an arms control process which for decades has been governed on the basis of U.S.-Soviet/Russian bilateral agreements. Even something as simple as extending the existing New START treaty for five years in order to buy time for the complexities of transitioning bilateral arms control structures into a new trilateral reality is unacceptable to Washington.

As insane as it might appear, the Trump approach might provide the only viable path forward regarding the possibility of meaningful trilateral arms control between the U.S., Russia, and China. As things currently stand, the failure to extend New START will eliminate constraints on the part of both the U.S. and Russia when it comes to fielding new strategic nuclear weapons. This alone is a destabilizing and dangerous reality which, left to its own devices, could lead to a new nuclear arms race which would make those of the Cold War pale in comparison in terms of capability and lethality. The wild card in this equation is China. Here, as things currently stand, the small size and relative lack of sophistication of China's existing strategic nuclear arsenal make it a virtual non-player when it comes to discussions of symmetrical disarmament based upon historical triad constructs (where strategic nuclear capability is spread among manned bombers, land-based ICBMs, and submarine-launched ballistic missiles.)

China's current nuclear force structure is heavily weighted toward intermediate-range missiles. However, any nuclear modernization program that saw China develop a viable triad-based nuclear deterrence capability would not only compel both Russia and the U.S. to take into account a Chinese strategic nuclear threat when building their respective post-New START nuclear force structure, but also create real political incentive on the part of all three nations to take the off-ramp from a path of nuclear posture escalation and instead embrace the de-escalation of trilateral arms control.

This, of course, is not the ideal situation. Trillions of dollars will be expended by all three parties pursuing weapons whose only utility is to create the conditions for their eventual elimination. But nuclear policy historically has not been the purview of sane and rational thinking—one only needs to refer to the deterrence model of "mutually assured destruction" (MAD) to make that point.

In the early 1980s both the U.S. and the Soviet Union knew that to escalate tensions by deploying new INF weapons into Europe was an inherently dangerous gambit. Indeed, on at least one occasion it nearly triggered a general nuclear war. But in the end, it was the only politically viable path toward eventual disarmament and the normalization of relations between the U.S. and the Soviet Union.

In the dangerous waters of a post-New START world, perhaps the only way to navigate clear of the rocks and shoals of nuclear conflict is for China to escalate its development of a viable strategic nuclear force to enable the kind of meaningful trilateral strategic nuclear arms control the world needs to survive.

[This article was originally published in *Russia Today* on May 12, 2020.]

CHAPTER FIFTEEN
North Korea Goes Ballistic

"They that sow the wind, shall reap the Whirlwind" is a proverbial phrase taken from the Old Testament, the Book of Hosea 8:7, which alludes to the notion that those who pursue false idols shall face the severity of God's judgment. There is no better phrase that captures the current reality of American arms control policy with North Korea, which for decades has been built on the dual objectives of containment and regime change.

This policy has collapsed in the face of sustained North Korean recalcitrance and defiance; North Korea today has a strategic nuclear weapons capability that is firmly attached to the survival of its regime. Any effort to remove the North Korean regime will result in the employment of these weapons in its defense; any effort to forcefully eliminate these weapons through military force will likewise result in their employment. Given the horrific consequences of any such action, that awful truth is that there simply is no military solution worthy of the name.

It is a little understood reality that it was the United States that first introduced nuclear weapons into the Korean Peninsula and, by including South Korea and Japan in its strategic nuclear umbrella, has made nuclear weapons an ever-present reality of any foreign policy or national security discussion on North Korea. The decision by the United States in 1957 to abrogate paragraph 13(d) of the Korean armistice agreement prohibiting the introduction of new weapons into the Korean Peninsula was seen as an economy of force measure by then-President Eisenhower, who believed that the deployment of nuclear weapons to South Korea would allow the United States to withdraw its large conventional military presence there. For North

Korea, it was seen as a direct threat to its existence, given the fact that the American policy at that time was, and continues to be, one that seeks regime change through containment and destabilization.

There is a linkage between arms control and regime change that has existed, and continues to exist, in America's post-Cold War foreign and national security policy calculations. This linkage is obvious, especially when it comes to nations that have been labeled by Washington as being "rogue" in nature. Iraq stands out in this regard; the efforts by UN weapons inspectors to disarm Iraq's weapons of mass destruction (WMD) were only useful to the United States in so far as it facilitated the removal of Saddam Hussein from power. The attack on Libya followed suit—the United States moved to eliminate Muammar Gaddafi's chemical and nuclear capabilities prior to overseeing his forceful eviction, and ultimate demise. Until President Trump's reversed course on American policy vis-à-vis the need for Syrian President Assad to step aside as a precondition for peace in that troubled nation, the efforts to disarm Syria of its chemical arsenal were viewed only in the light of defanging a threat before eliminating it.

Regime change in Pyongyang has always underpinned American policy toward North Korea. North Korea's considerable conventional military capability, combined with the proximity of China and a history of Chinese military intervention when North Korean sovereignty was violated, has meant that the United States has pursued a non-kinetic solution, focusing on economic containment and diplomatic isolation to compel internal unrest that could lead to the peaceful transition of power within North Korea, and eventually the unification of Korea as a singular political entity governed out of Seoul.

When, in the 1980s, North Korea undertook to develop an indigenous nuclear capability, the United States treated this initiative as a subset of its larger policy of containment and isolation. America never really negotiated in good faith. North Korea was never given any

Chapter Fifteen: *North Korea Goes Ballistic*

options other than that which furthered American policy objectives of containment and isolation by denying North Korea the ability to meaningfully integrate with its neighbors and the rest of the world.

This policy of economic and diplomatic isolation of North Korea did produce two dividends to the detriment of American policy—it strengthened the resolve of Pyongyang to build an economy hardened against the pressures of economic sanctions, and it produced a paranoia within the North Korean leadership that turned every military move by the United States in the region into a direct threat to North Korea itself. History has shown us the results: Economic sanctions have proven incapable of compelling change within North Korea, and North Korea has perfected a long-range ballistic missile delivery system and a miniaturized nuclear payload that brings parts of the United States into range.

There are no good options for resolving the unfolding crisis with North Korea. There is no viable military option worthy of the name—the United States simply lacks the concentration of conventional military power in the region to conduct the kind of broad-spectrum, sustained interdiction required for successful preemption of any North Korean attack. Significant North Korean forces, both conventional and strategic, would survive. The devastation of Seoul through conventional artillery fire would all but be assured, along with the real potential of a nuclear missile attack on South Korea, Japan, and the territory of the United States. In short, an American preemptive military strike would only accelerate a North Korean nuclear attack.

Total diplomatic capitulation in the face of North Korean intransigence is likewise an unacceptable outcome. It would preserve the North Korean nuclear and strategic missile capability as an unconstrained reality, embolden North Korean action on the Korean peninsula and beyond, while exposing as impotent both America's conventional and nuclear military deterrence capability. Moreover, both South Korea and Japan would likely embark on building their own independent nuclear deterrence, undermining American and international objectives on nuclear nonproliferation.

Stuck between two unacceptable options, the United States will need to think out of the box in its search for a solution to the North Korean nuclear conundrum. One thing not being considered is the strengthening of economic sanctions targeting either North Korea or those who continue to trade with Pyongyang. Sanctions represent little more than the antithesis of policy and have played a significant role in boxing the United States in a corner when it comes to resolving the issue of North Korean nuclear capability. Moreover, a policy of seeking to punish China as a means of garnering Chinese support is inherently counterintuitive.

China is the key to any solution. At this juncture, the United States has little choice but to accept the reality of North Korea's nuclear armament. The problem now becomes how best to contain this reality, and eventually roll it back. One solution would be to turn to the Chinese and invite them to extend their nuclear umbrella over North Korea, incorporating the North Korean nuclear arsenal into a unified nuclear deterrence capability. China would announce a no first use policy, which would extend to the North Korean nuclear force. Any unilateral violation of this policy by North Korea would result in the Chinese nuclear umbrella being automatically withdrawn. The North Korean strategic nuclear force would be capped at an agreed level, perhaps a regiment-sized force of some dozen missiles.

The United States could then enter into serious arms control discussions with China that included North Korea and Russia (and later India and Pakistan) to scale back the size of their respective nuclear arsenals (understanding that Chinese nuclear disarmament cannot take place in a regional vacuum). One of the key objectives of any such negotiation would be a freeze on the deployment of nuclear

Chapter Fifteen: *North Korea Goes Ballistic*

weapons and their delivery systems by all parties, and the institution of on-site inspections as a means of verifying compliance; this would get American eyes on the North Korean arsenal, increasing confidence among American politicians that North Korea was not operating in violation of the accord. (It would also halt a trillion-dollar nuclear modernization program currently planned for the American nuclear arsenal.)

The nuclear negotiations could go hand in hand with a larger regional conference on stability in the Korean Peninsula which would involve the reduction of conventional military forces on both sides of the demilitarized zone, the removal of destabilizing weaponry, such as the American THAAD anti-missile capability and North Korean medium-range missiles, and the normalization of economic relations between North Korea and its regional neighbors, free of sanctions. The endgame in this dual approach would be to create a situation where North Korea would no longer feel the necessity to possess an independent strategic nuclear capability, and instead be willing to exist under the protection of a Chinese nuclear deterrence force that would, over time, be negotiated down to zero, along with the other nuclear arsenals of the world.

This kind of creative diplomacy has been lacking over the years, mainly due to the arrogance on the part of American diplomats and policy formulators that blinded them to the good of the global collective in the name of sustaining unilateral American nuclear supremacy. The American struggle to maintain its place at the top of the world's power structure has, at times, taken on machinations that would rival "Game of Thrones" in conspiratorial complexity. "Chaos is a Ladder" may work as a policy thematic in fantasy, but in reality, it is a recipe for disaster, as the current American policy failure with North Korea underscores. It is high time Washington divorces itself from decades of failed policy formulation and instead embark on a new path that leads to a resolution that offers something other than American supremacy at the cost of regional and global instability.

• • •

Over the course of the past decade, North Korea has developed a robust indigenous ballistic missile production capability that has produced a wide range of advanced weapons systems, including short-range, intermediate-range, intercontinental ballistic missiles (ICBMs), submarine-launched missiles and—most recently—hypersonic missiles. When armed with nuclear weapons, these missiles present a credible deterrent to potential regional adversaries, including the U.S., South Korea and Japan. Although the principle of mutually assured destruction precludes North Korea from implementing a policy of preemptive nuclear attack, advances in missile technology, when combined with new North Korean satellite surveillance capabilities, give Pyongyang a conventional strike capability that could most likely defeat existing U.S. ballistic missile defenses. The U.S. and its regional partners must now factor in the possibility of a debilitating North Korean preemptive attack that could alter the strategic balance of power in ways never envisioned by the West.

North Korea has made some significant progress with its missile program in recent months. On January 14, it conducted a test launch of a two-stage, intermediate-range, solid-fuel ballistic missile loaded with a hypersonic maneuverable controlled warhead. The purpose of the test was to verify the operational characteristics of the warhead and the reliability of the solid rocket engines, believed to be comprised of the first two stages of the North Korean Hwasong-18 three-stage solid-fueled ICBM.

Then, on March 20, North Korea conducted a static test of a second-stage rocket motor intended for use on the Hwasong-16B hypersonic missile. This test was intended to confirm the performance of its second stage. Unlike a conventional ballistic missile, which uses the characteristics of parabolic motion defined by the impact of the earth's gravity on an object to reach a designated target (often at velocities that are many times the speed of sound), a hypersonic missile uses the power of its propulsion system, independent of gravitational forces, to achieve speeds in excess of five times the speed of sound (the lower limit of what can be classified as hypersonic speed).

This was followed, on April 2, by the launch of a Hwongsong-16B intermediate-range missile equipped with the hypersonic maneuverable controlled warhead that had been flight tested on January 14. This missile used the solid rocket booster of the Hwasong-18 ICBM, the hypersonic-capable second stage that had been static tested on March 20, and the new maneuverable warhead which, when combined, gives North Korea an operational intermediate-range hypersonic missile capability.

While the U.S. and South Korea have questioned some of the performance characteristics cited by North Korea regarding the test of the Hwasong-16B, the fact is that the rapid pace of the testing involved, and North Korea's ability to seamlessly integrate systems into an operational platform, is an impressive accomplishment—indeed, so impressive that one must question whether North Korea received outside assistance from either Russia, China or both. Although North Korea had previously tested an intermediate-range hypersonic missile in 2021, that system used liquid fuel. Liquid fuel, because of its highly corrosive nature, cannot be loaded onto a missile airframe until just before the missile is to be launched. This increases the reaction time of the weapon and makes it vulnerable to detection and interdiction during the fueling process. Solid-fueled missiles can be launched without any advance preparation, increasing the threat posed by such weapons and their survivability on a modern battlefield.

North Korea has, over the course of more than a decade, developed an array of ballistic missile capabilities, including short-, intermediate- and intercontinental-ranged systems, as well as missiles that can be launched from submarines. The primary threat posed by these missiles against any potential adversary, such as the U.S., Japan and South Korea, is their role as a delivery vehicle for a North Korean nuclear weapon.

North Korea's nuclear weapons capability, however, is widely acknowledged to be part of a larger policy of deterrence, as opposed to representing a first-strike capability. North Korea is certainly aware of the nuclear capabilities of the U.S., and the reality that any use of nuclear weapons by North Korea would result in a nuclear response that would effectively destroy it as a viable nation state. The mutually assured destruction aspect of this balance of power is intended to forestall any non-nuclear first strike by the U.S. and its regional allies intended to "decapitate" the North Korean leadership, something the U.S. and South Korea have not only announced is part of their range of military options regarding North Korea, but one that is also regularly tested in joint training exercises.

The development of an operational intermediate-range hypersonic missile capability by North Korea changes this balance of power dramatically. The ability to launch on short notice a weapon system than can reach its target in minutes, while evading existing ballistic missile defense systems, when combined with North Korean satellite surveillance capabilities that allow for rapid target identification, gives North Korea the ability to launch its own conventional preemptive strike. Such a strike, if carried out against airfields, ports, and command and control facilities, could cripple U.S., South Korean and Japanese military capabilities prior to a possible invasion of South Korea. North Korea's nuclear arsenal would prevent a U.S. nuclear

Chapter Fifteen: *North Korea Goes Ballistic*

response, creating a possible scenario where North Korea could defeat U.S. and South Korean forces on the Korean peninsula.

The U.S. has downplayed the threat posed by North Korea's missiles—including its new hypersonic weapon—citing the ballistic missile defense capabilities that it has in the region, alongside those of South Korea and Japan. The ballistic missile defense architecture that the U.S. has deployed in the region includes advanced ground-based radars, including the AN/TPY-2 X-band radar, and the most modern missile interceptors in the U.S. arsenal, including the THAAD and Patriot 3. These systems are joined by Aegis-equipped navy vessels from both the U.S. and Japan, with advanced S-band radars and modern SM-3 missile interceptors. These systems are linked into a global ballistic missile defense architecture that incorporates satellites and other technologies to provide the U.S., South Korea and Japan the ability to detect any North Korean missile launch, track the missile inflight and destroy it before it can reach its intended target.

The problem with the U.S. posture is that the recent missile attack by Iran on Israel has shown the ballistic missile defense architecture that the U.S. is relying on for the defense of the Korean Peninsula and surrounding region to be fallible. In Israel, the U.S. deployed a ballistic missile defense architecture that incorporated all the systems it has available in South Korea, Japan and the surrounding regions. The Israeli architecture was further reinforced by an extensive ballistic defense shield jointly developed by the U.S. and Israel.

The number of Iranian missiles getting through the missile shield to strike targets inside Israel is undetermined at this juncture, but more than the five officially acknowledged.

The Iranian missiles—although a generation removed from the new North Korean hypersonic missile—employed maneuvering warheads and warheads equipped with decoys to foil the U.S.-Israeli ballistic missile defense architecture. U.S. military planners, and those of its allies that rely on U.S. missile defense systems for their protection, must re-evaluate operational assumptions premised on the notion of protection that cannot be guaranteed.

[This chapter is comprised of two articles: "Resolving North Korea Without 'Fire and Fury,'" published in *The American Conservative*, August 10, 2017, and "North Korea goes Ballistic," published in *Energy Intelligence*, April 23, 2024.]

CHAPTER SIXTEEN
The Israeli-Iranian Nuclear Conundrum

President Trump made it official Tuesday, announcing that he would be withdrawing from the Iran nuclear agreement, officially known as the Joint Comprehensive Program of Action, or JCPOA. "The agreement," he said in his speech, "was so poorly negotiated that even if Iran fully complies, the regime can still be on the verge of a nuclear breakout in just a short period of time. The deal's sunset provisions are totally unacceptable. If I allowed this deal to stand, there would soon be a nuclear arms race in the Middle East."

The sunset provisions of the JCPOA are among the least understood aspects of that agreement. Prior to signing the JCPOA, Iran operated more than 20,000 centrifuges for enriching uranium to use in its indigenous nuclear program. The level of enrichment attained—3.7 percent for nuclear power reactors and under 20 percent for use in a medical research reactor—was well below that needed for use in a nuclear weapon. However, the international community, led by the United States, was concerned that Iran would be able to use its large number of centrifuges to rapidly increase the level of enrichment of its uranium stockpile to more than 90 percent, allowing Iran to have the fissile material needed for a nuclear bomb (or bombs) in a very short time.

In the lexicon of the nonproliferation specialists monitoring Iran, a new term was coined—"breakout time." This was the amount of time required for Iran, once inspectors from the International Atomic Energy Agency (IAEA) who were monitoring its nuclear enrichment efforts were removed, to produce enough 90 percent-enriched uranium to make a nuclear bomb. Using the 20,000 centrifuges it possessed, Iran's breakout time was estimated to be around three months if using natural uranium feedstock, or around four weeks if using uranium feedstock already enriched to 3.7 percent.

The collective wisdom in the arms control community was that Iran needed to be kept to a breakout time of no less than one year. Under the JCPOA, this would be done by limiting the number of centrifuges it could operate to just over 5,000, while limiting the amount of 3.7 percent-enriched uranium it could have stored at any given time to no more than 300 kilograms. With these restrictions in place, Iran would have a breakout time of more than one year.

But for Iran, agreeing to such limitations in perpetuity made little sense. One of the considerations given to JCPOA calculus was that Iran eventually would seek to build an indigenous nuclear energy production capability, and it would require modern centrifuges capable of generating quantities of enriched uranium far in excess of 300 kilograms. Indeed, one of the key aspects of the JCPOA is Iran's "long-term enrichment and enrichment research and development plan," which details how Iran will proceed during the life of the JCPOA to prepare for the eventual implementation of a large-scale uranium enrichment program that would far exceed the parameters of the 12-month breakout scenario set forth in the main body of the JCPOA.

The so-called sunset clause of the JCPOA holds that after 15 years—meaning by 2030—all restrictions on the number of centrifuges Iran is allowed to operate, as well as the amount of enriched uranium it is permitted to store, will be lifted. In addition to increasing the numbers of centrifuges Iran can operate, it also will be able to start using more efficient, modern centrifuges.

For Iran, this clears the way to replace the inefficient centrifuges it can possess and operate under the JCPOA with as many highly

Chapter Sixteen: *The Israeli-Iranian Nuclear Conundrum*

efficient modern centrifuges as it deems necessary to meet its legitimate needs for nuclear energy. The JCPOA allows for Iran to begin replacing its older centrifuges with more capable models between years 11 and 13 of the agreement. Given the improved performance characteristics of these newer centrifuges, the one-year breakout time would be reduced to around four months sometime between years 11 and 13 of the JCPOA, or as early as 2026. It is this inevitable demise of the 12-month breakout window that prompted Trump to walk away from the JCPOA on the grounds that it no longer served U.S. national security interests.

Trump, however, was not the author of the JCPOA. That "honor" fell to President Barack Obama. On the issue of Iran, Obama proved as disingenuous as his predecessor, George W. Bush, when it came to fact-based policy on Iraq. A 2007 National Intelligence Estimate on Iran's nuclear program concluded that Iran had not conducted any work on a nuclear weapon since 2003, and that intelligence provided to the IAEA by Israel in 2004 (which purported to prove the existence of a covert Iranian nuclear program) turned out to be of questionable provenance. The Obama administration, however, encouraged the IAEA in 2011 to release a report based upon the same discredited 2004 Israeli documents. The sole purpose of this report was to build consensus within the United States and around the world for the passage of stringent economic sanctions against Iran designed to pressure Tehran into giving up its nuclear program.

While Obama was able to use the 2011 IAEA report to push through Congress new unilateral American sanctions targeting Iranian oil sales in early 2012 (these sanctions were then used to pressure other countries to halt their purchase of Iranian oil through so-called secondary sanctions, which punished anyone operating in violation of U.S. law), it failed in forcing Iran to the negotiating table.

With everything the U.S. and its allies threw at Iran, including having Iranian citizens pay a huge economic cost in terms of a devastated economy and reduced quality of life, the pressure campaign still failed. The U.S.-led economic sanctions, rather than forcing Iran to abandon its nuclear program, empowered it to expand it efforts dramatically. The consequence was a dangerous situation. The U.S., after falsely building a narrative of Iran aggressively pursuing a nuclear weapon, now needed to either militarily confront Iran (and its expanding enrichment capacity) or find a diplomatic way out of a self-inflicted wound without losing political face at home and abroad.

The JCPOA was the result—a deal that recognized Iran's right to enrich uranium for peaceful purposes (something the U.S. opposed for decades) while backing away from the fiction that it was pursuing a nuclear weapons program. The IAEA, the U.S. and every nation that embraced the falsified intelligence used to underpin the allegations of an Iranian nuclear weapons program—so-called possible military dimensions, or PMD—could not acknowledge that what they sold to the world was founded on lies, so they constructed an inelegant solution. The IAEA, after consulting with Iran, prepared a report that "resolved" the PMD problem once and for all, and thus paved the way for the lifting of economic sanctions.

Yes, Iran agreed to an unprecedented level of intrusive inspections and restrictions on its enrichment program. But the JCPOA's bottom line is that Iran retained thousands of active centrifuges in full operation. This represented a major political victory for Iran, given the years-long, concerted, U.S.-led effort to deny it access to even a single spinning centrifuge. No matter how hard the Obama administration tried to sell the JCPOA as a victory for American diplomacy and international peace and security, Iran brought the U.S. to the negotiating table, emerging with a nuclear program the world had tried to prevent

Chapter Sixteen: *The Israeli-Iranian Nuclear Conundrum*

it from obtaining while giving up a fictional nuclear weapons program it neither possessed nor desired.

The JCPOA was made to resolve a difficult and dangerous situation the U.S. created for itself. As a result, the Obama administration had to craft an agreement built on a foundation of lies. These lies proved to be its undoing. If Iran, as the U.S. claimed in pushing for economic sanctions, possessed a nuclear weapons program, and no effort was made to ensure that it acknowledged and dismantled that program, then any agreement delaying Iran access to the ability to produce enough highly enriched uranium for use in a nuclear weapon kicked Iran's inevitable acquisition of a nuclear bomb down the road.

This is the heart of Trump's argument against the JCPOA: that the so-called sunset clauses limiting the number and quality of Iranian centrifuges only delay, rather than prevent, an Iranian nuclear weapons program from reaching fruition. To alter Trump's logic, the U.S. would need to discredit the intelligence it used to justify the economic sanctions it suspended when signing the JCPOA—the same sanctions the U.S. threatened to "snap back" in place if Iran was found to be in violation, and that Trump reinstated when he pulled out of the agreement.

The U.S. failed to do this, and the onus for this failure rests solely with the Obama administration. To save political face by not having to acknowledge that the heart of its Iran policy was built on a foundation of lies, the Obama administration embedded this lie into the heart of the JCPOA in the form of the agreement to resolve the "possible military dimension" issue based upon a wink and a nod, as opposed to verifiable inspections. While this was done as a political expedient designed to breathe life into the JCPOA, it turned out to be a poison pill that killed the agreement. One need only witness the briefing by Israeli Prime Minister Benjamin Netanyahu, in which he cites a newly acquired archive of Iranian documents detailing an alleged nuclear weapons program, and the extent to which Trump relied on that presentation to underpin his decision to leave the JCPOA.

Trump will go down in history as the man who walked away from an agreement that all parties—including the U.S.—acknowledge that Iran was fully compliant with. Trump only deludes himself and those who support him by saying that his actions to confront a threat from Iran now, rather than waiting for it to manifest itself, will make America more secure. Iran's nuclear program poses no threat to either America or the world, because it is, and always has been, a peaceful civilian program, something those in power know to be the case.

Trump was able to exploit the lies the Obama administration perpetrated in justifying his decision to walk away from the JCPOA. That fact is a sad reflection of the level of ignorance and antipathy that exists among U.S. citizens and those they elect to represent them in Congress.

Congress is, and has been, a witting facilitator of these lies. This should come as no surprise, however, because those the American people elect are a reflection of those they represent. Since 1979, when an Iranian mob took over the U.S. Embassy in Tehran and held 52 Americans hostage for more than 400 days, the American people have been programmed to accept all information that paints Iran and its theocratic government in a negative light. When President Obama said Iran had a nuclear weapons program, the American people—even after the previous administration's lies about weapons of mass destruction in Iraq—did not demand hard evidence to back up the accusation.

Democrats will blame Trump for walking away from the JCPOA, and Republicans will blame Obama for making such a bad deal. But Congress, empowered by an ignorant American public willing to swallow at face value any news that paints Iran in a bad light, has made all of this possible. A lack of meaningful oversight of the intelligence community has allowed the lies about Iranian nuclear capability to be

Chapter Sixteen: *The Israeli-Iranian Nuclear Conundrum*

promulgated. Those lies were then used to impose economic sanctions intended to compel Iran to abandon a program it was not pursuing.

When examined from this perspective, Trump's actions are a logical extension of the collective will of the American people, expressed over time through the actions of Congress. True, Obama gave us the nuclear agreement with Iran, despite its political unpopularity with Congress as a whole. Like all policies built on a foundation of lies, though, the JCPOA was doomed from its inception. Eventually, the incompatible notion of a fictional Iranian nuclear weapons ambition sold by Obama to Congress would collide with the reality of a renewed Iranian enrichment capacity once the sunset clauses of the JCPOA expired.

We can point the finger at Trump all we want, but at the end of the day, the American people—Republicans, Democrats, Independents and all others—share collective responsibility for his decision to walk away from the Iranian nuclear agreement. It conforms to a set of facts most Americans embraced, unquestioning, in endorsing a policy of economic containment that backfired.

Trump's actions in walking away from the JCPOA didn't shred American credibility. That happened a long time ago, before Donald J. Trump was even a glimmer in the eye of those who elected him.

• • •

As the war between Israel and Hamas enters its second month, one of the top priorities of all parties involved is to prevent the conflict from expanding regionally. Israeli concerns over the emergence of a northern front with Hezbollah along Israel's border with Lebanon have prompted the U.S. to deploy significant military power to the eastern Mediterranean Sea as a show of force to deter both Hezbollah and Iran from intervening. The prospect of a larger war between Israel and Iran has also shone an uncomfortable light on Israel's nuclear weapons capability, and the possibility of these weapons being used if the fighting in Gaza were to expand regionally. Both Israel and the U.S. have accused Iran of pursuing a covert nuclear weapons program, which Iran vehemently denies.

Recent comments by Israeli Heritage Minister Amichai Eliyahu, where he alluded to the possibility that one of Israel's options in the war against Hamas could be to use nuclear weapons in the Gaza Strip, thrust the reality of Israel's unacknowledged nuclear weapons program into the international spotlight. Eliyahu's comments were quickly disavowed by Israeli Prime Minister Benjamin Netanyahu, and the heritage minister was suspended from attending cabinet meetings.

Eliyahu, a member of National Security Minister Itamar Ben Gvir's far-right Otzma Yehudit (Jewish Power) party, made his comments while answering a question during a live radio interview. "Your expectation is that tomorrow morning we'd drop what amounts to some kind of a nuclear bomb on all of Gaza, flattening them, eliminating everybody there?" the interviewer asked. "That's one way," Eliyahu responded.

It should be noted that Eliyahu never mentioned nuclear weapons himself. Likewise, the questioner did not speak of an actual nuclear weapon, but rather something "that amounts to" a nuclear weapon. Many observers of the ongoing Gaza conflict have made comparisons with the volume of high explosives that have been dropped on Gaza by the Israeli Air Force since October 7, [2023] when Hamas launched a surprise attack on Israeli military and civilian infrastructure surrounding Gaza, killing some 1,400 Israelis, most of them civilians. The tonnage dropped on Gaza is estimated at more than 20,000 tons, the equivalent of a 20-kiloton nuclear bomb, which is larger than either of the atomic bombs dropped by the U.S. on the Japanese cities of Hiroshima and Nagasaki at the end of World War II.

Chapter Sixteen: *The Israeli-Iranian Nuclear Conundrum*

That the mere allusion to the existence and possible use of nuclear weapons by an Israeli government official, however vague and indistinct, could attract such attention underscores the controversy that surrounds Israel's nuclear weapons program.

The Israeli nuclear weapons program dates to the mid-1950s, when the country's first prime minister, David Ben-Gurion, ordered the Israeli military to develop a nuclear insurance plan designed to offset the combined conventional military superiority of Israel's Arab neighbors. Developed in great secrecy with the assistance of France, the Israeli program was centered on a nuclear weapons production facility located at Dimona, in the Negev Desert, where Israel, under the guise of a civilian nuclear power program, began to produce the plutonium necessary for a nuclear weapon.

U.S. President John F. Kennedy confronted Ben-Gurion about Dimona during a May 1961 meeting. Under pressure, Ben-Gurion stated that the Dimona plant had a pilot plutonium extraction capability that could be used for military purposes but sought to mollify U.S. concerns by declaring that Israel had "no intention to develop weapons capacity now."

The administration of President Richard Nixon subsequently worked with Israel to craft a policy of mutual obfuscation, where Israel promised that it would not be the first to "introduce" nuclear weapons to the Middle East, but premised this on the notion that the term "introduce" meant the acknowledgement of the existence of such a weapon—in short, "introduction" was not about physical possession, but about public acknowledgment of that possession.

While Israel has sought to assiduously maintain its policy of nuclear ambiguity, there have been some notable incidents that strain the credulity of this posture. In 2004, while speaking at a political party gathering in Tel Aviv, Israeli Prime Minister Ariel Sharon made an indirect comparison between the nuclear ambitions, real and imagined, of Libya and Iran, which he indicated should be halted, and Israel, which Sharon said, "must not be touched when it comes to its deterrent capability."

In a December 2006 interview with German television, Sharon's successor, Ehud Olmert, appeared to openly acknowledge Israel's nuclear status when he criticized Iran for aspiring "to have nuclear weapons, as America, France, Israel, Russia."

In 1986 Mordechai Vanunu, an Israeli nuclear technician who had been employed at the Dimona facility, went public with information about the technical capacity of Israel to produce the fissile material necessary for nuclear weapons. The Stockholm International Peace Research Institute currently estimates that Israel's nuclear arsenal consists of 80 weapons—50 for delivery using ballistic missiles, and 30 for delivery by aircraft. Israel is also believed to possess an unknown number of nuclear artillery shells and atomic demolition munitions.

How Israel might transition from its posture of nuclear ambiguity to being a self-declared nuclear state remains unknown. However, given Israel's close collaboration with South Africa over the development and probable testing of nuclear weapons, the South African model of making its nuclear deterrence public is likely to resemble Israel's approach. This involves a three-phase strategy, with phase one being nuclear ambiguity. Phase two involves what is known as covert conditioning, involving a variety of non-attributable methods to reveal nuclear capacity as a means of inducement, persuasion and/or coercion. The third phase involves overtly acknowledging possession of weapons capability, followed by a series of escalating steps—public announcement, public display, demonstration (e.g. a nuclear test), threatened use, and lastly, battlefield use.

In the aftermath of the October 7 attack by Hamas, Israel faces a crisis that its senior-most leadership describes as existential in nature. In 2022 and 2023, Israel carried out large-scale military exercises designed to test the Israel Defense Forces' ability to respond to simultaneous attacks from all known enemies of Israel—Hamas, Hezbollah, Syria and Iran. While the official results of these exercises remain a state secret, some conclusions have been alluded to by Israeli military sources. First, any military conflict between Israel and Iran could only be conducted with significant military assistance from the U.S., which might not be forthcoming. Second, Hezbollah possesses sufficient missile capacity to overwhelm Israeli air defenses, enabling them to inflict serious harm to Israeli economic, political and military infrastructure. Thirdly, the Israeli exercises did not envision a major attack by Hamas that would consume so much of Israel's conventional military power in response.

If the current conflict with Hamas were to escalate to involve both Hezbollah and Iran, Israel most probably lacks the conventional military capability to defeat this combined threat. At this juncture, Israel would face the decision of initiating the third phase of its nuclear deterrent posture: overt acknowledgement followed by escalatory steps. The decision to publicly declare an Israeli nuclear capability is a matter of great political sensitivity which, if done improperly, could turn even its U.S. ally against it. This is why Israeli Prime Minister Benjamin Netanyahu responded so harshly to the indiscreet ruminations of an obscure Israeli minister. Any step of this magnitude must be conducted in a very controlled fashion, with very specific objectives in mind—all of which should be linked to deterring the potential for operational use, not encouraging it.

[This chapter is composed of two articles: "Iran Nuclear Deal and U.S. Pullout Reflect Epic Bipartisan Failures," originally published in *TruthDig*, May 12, 2018, and "Israel's Nuclear Weapons in the Spotlight," originally published in *Energy Intelligence*, Nov. 13, 2023.]

PART FIVE

The Arms Race, Part Two

CHAPTER SEVENTEEN
Nuclear High Noon in Europe

On Monday, October 17, 2022, the North Atlantic Treaty Organization kicked off Operation STEADFAST NOON, its annual exercise of its ability to wage nuclear conflict. Given that NATO's nuclear umbrella extends exclusively over Europe, the indisputable fact is that STEADFAST NOON is nothing more than NATO training to wage nuclear war against Russia.

Nuclear war against Russia.

The reader should let that sink in for a moment.

Don't worry, NATO spokesperson Oana Lungscu reassured the rest of the world, the purpose of STEADFAST NOON is to ensure that NATO's nuclear war-fighting capability "remains safe and effective." It is a "routine" exercise, not linked to any current world events. Moreover, no "real" nuclear weapons will be used—just "fake" ones.

Nothing to worry about here.

Enter Jens Stoltenberg, NATO secretary general, stage right in the nuclear theater. In a statement to the press on October 11, Stoltenberg declared that, "Russia's victory in the war against Ukraine will be a defeat of NATO," before ominously announcing, "This cannot be allowed."

To that end, Stoltenberg stated, the STEADFAST NOON nuclear drills would continue as scheduled. These drills, Stoltenberg said, were an important deterrence mechanism in the face of Russian "veiled nuclear threats."

But they weren't related to any current world events.

Enter Volodymyr Zelensky, stage left. Speaking to the Lowy Institute, a nonpartisan international policy think tank in Australia, the Ukrainian president called for the international community to undertake "preventative strikes, preventive action" against Russia to deter the potential use of nuclear weapons by Russia against Ukraine.

While many observers interpreted Zelensky's words to imply a request for NATO to carry out a preemptive nuclear strike against Russia, Zelensky's aides were quick to try and correct the record, saying he was simply asking for more sanctions.

Enter Joe Biden, center stage. Speaking at a fundraiser on October 6, the president of the United States said that, "For the first time since the Cuban missile crisis, we have a direct threat of the use of a nuclear weapon if in fact things continue down the path they are going."

Biden went on: "We've got a guy I know fairly well. He's not joking when he talks about potential use of tactical nuclear weapons or biological or chemical weapons because his military is, you might say, significantly underperforming."

Biden concluded: "I don't think there's any such thing as the ability to easily use a tactical nuclear weapon and not end up with Armageddon."

While it has been made abundantly clear by the White House that Biden's comments were his personal view, and not based on any new intelligence regarding Russian nuclear posture, the fact that a sitting U.S. president was speaking about the possibility of a nuclear "Armageddon" should send chills down the spine of every sane individual in the world.

First and foremost, there has been zero talk about the employment of tactical nuclear weapons from the Kremlin.

Zero.

Russian President Vladimir Putin has indicated that Russia would use "all the means at its disposal" to protect Russia. He said this most recently on September 21, [2022] when in a televised address announcing partial mobilization, he accused the West of engaging in "nuclear blackmail," citing "statements of some high-ranking

Chapter Seventeen: *Nuclear High Noon in Europe*

representatives of the leading NATO states about the possibility of using nuclear weapons of mass destruction against Russia."

Putin was alluding to a statement that Liz Truss made prior to her election as British prime minister, when, in response to a question on whether she was ready to undertake the responsibility of ordering the use of the U.K.'s nuclear arsenal, she replied, "I think it's an important duty of the prime minister and I'm ready to do that."

"I want to remind you," Putin said, "that our country also has various means of destruction and in some components more modern than those of the NATO countries. And if the territorial integrity of our country is threatened, we will certainly use all the means at our disposal to protect Russia and our people."

Putin's statements were consistent with that of Russian Defense Minister Sergei Shoigu, who in an address to the 10th Moscow Conference on International Security delivered on August 16, asserted that Russia would not use nuclear weapons in Ukraine. According to Shoigu, Russian nuclear weapons are authorized for use under "exceptional circumstances" as described in published Russian doctrine, none of which apply to the Ukraine situation. Any talk of the use of nuclear weapons by Russia in Ukraine, Shoigu said, was "absurd."

Apparently not to Biden, who despite his claim to know Putin "fairly well," got it all wrong when talking about the potential for nuclear conflict.

The risk isn't that Russia would start a pre-emptive nuclear war over Ukraine.

The risk is that America would.

Biden came into office in February 2021 promising to enshrine in U.S. nuclear doctrine a "sole purpose policy," under which "the sole purpose of our nuclear arsenal should be to deter—and, if necessary, retaliate against—a nuclear attack."

It is now the middle of October 2022, and America finds itself in a situation where the president himself fears for a potential nuclear "Armageddon."

If ever there was a time for Biden to make good on his pledge, now is it.

But he remains silent.

The danger inherent in Biden's silence is that Putin and other Russian officials who are concerned about Russian national security must rely upon existing published U.S. nuclear doctrine, which continues to enshrine a policy of nuclear pre-emption promulgated during the administration of President George W. Bush. Under this doctrine, nuclear weapons are but another tool in the military's toolbox, to be used as and when needed, including occasions where the destruction of battlefield targets for the simple purpose of gaining an operational advantage is the objective.

One can argue that this sort of non-nuclear preemption has its own inherent deterrence value, a sort of "madman" kind of vibe that makes an opponent question whether the president could act in such an irrational manner.

"I call it the Madman Theory," former U.S. President Richard Nixon reportedly told his assistant, Bob Haldeman, during the Vietnam War. "I want the North Vietnamese to believe that I've reached the point that I might do anything to stop the war. We'll just slip the word to them that 'for God's sake, you know Nixon is obsessed about Communism. We can't restrain him when he's angry—and he has his hand on the nuclear button'—and Ho Chi Minh himself will be in Paris in two days begging for peace."

Former President Donald Trump breathed new life into Nixon's "madman theory," telling North Korea that if it continued to threaten the United States "[t]hey will be met with fire, fury and frankly power the likes of which this world has never seen before." Trump went on to have three face-to-face meetings with North Korean leader Kim Jong Un in a failed effort to bring about the denuclearization of the Korean Peninsula.

It was under the Trump administration that the U.S. Navy deployed the W-76-2 low-yield nuclear warhead on its Trident submarine-launched ballistic missiles, giving the president a greater range of options when it came to the employment of nuclear weapons.

"This supplemental capability," John Rood, the then-undersecretary of defense for policy, declared, "strengthens deterrence and provides the United States a prompt, more survivable low-yield strategic weapon; supports our commitment to extended deterrence; and demonstrates to potential adversaries that there is no advantage to limited nuclear employment because the United States can credibly and decisively respond to any threat scenario."

One such threat scenario that was tested involved the theoretical employment of a W-76-2 low-yield warhead in a Baltic European scenario in which targets from the actual wartime contingency were used as a point of illustration. In short, the U.S. trained to preemptively use the W-76-2 to compel Russia to back down (deescalate) lest they risk a nuclear escalation resulting in a general nuclear exchange—in short, Armageddon.

Which brings us to the present time. As this article is being written, U.S. nuclear-capable B-52 bombers are flying to Europe from their U.S. bases, where they will practice delivering nuclear weapons against a Russian target. Dozens more aircraft, flying from Volkel Air Force Base in the Netherlands (home to an arsenal of U.S. B-61 nuclear bombs), will practice employing NATO nuclear weapons against...Russia.

Russia has responded to the NATO nuclear drill by going forward with its own annual nuclear exercise, "Grom" (Thunder). These drills will involve the large-scale maneuver of Russia's strategic nuclear forces, including live missile launches. In a statement unmatched in its hypocrisy, a U.S. defense official, speaking on condition of anonymity, said "Russian nuclear rhetoric and its decision to proceed with this exercise while at war with Ukraine is irresponsible. Brandishing nuclear weapons to coerce the United States and its allies is irresponsible."

October 22, 1962—nearly 60 years ago to the day, President John F. Kennedy delivered a dramatic 18-minute television speech to the American people during which he revealed "unmistakable evidence" of the missile threat. Kennedy went on to announce that the United States would prevent ships carrying weapons from reaching Cuba and demanded that the Soviets withdraw their missiles.

At the same time, the U.S. ambassador to the Soviet Union, Foy Kohler, delivered a letter from Kennedy to Soviet Premier Nikita Khrushchev, saying "the one thing that has most concerned me has been the possibility that your government would not correctly understand the will and determination of the United States in any given situation, since I have not assumed that you or any other sane man would, in this nuclear age, deliberately plunge the world into war which it is crystal clear no country could win and which could only result in catastrophic consequences to the whole world, including the aggressor."

Joe Biden would do well to reflect on that letter, and all that transpired after that, and understand that if you replace "United States" with "Russia," one gets an accurate assessment of the current world view of Russia when it comes to NATO and nuclear weapons.

Now is not the time for drama, or theatrically inflammatory rhetoric. Now is the time for maturity, sanity…restraint. A sage leader would have recognized the possibility of misperception on the part of Russia when NATO, a mere week after being encouraged by the Ukrainian president to initiate a preemptive nuclear strike on Russia,

Chapter Seventeen: *Nuclear High Noon in Europe*

carries out a major exercise where NATO practices dropping nuclear bombs on Russia. A sober leader would have postponed these drills and encouraged similar action from Russia regarding its nuclear exercises.

Instead, America gets an unscripted, off-the-cuff reference to a nuclear Armageddon from a narcissistic egomaniac who uses the horror of nuclear annihilation as a fundraising mantra.

It would take but one miscalculation, a single misunderstanding to turn STEADFAST NOON into "High Noon," and "Grom" (Thunder) into "Molnya" (Lightening).

We've seen this scenario before. In November 1983 NATO carried out a command post exercise, codenamed ABLE ARCHER '83, designed to test "nuclear weapons release procedures." The Soviets were so alarmed by this exercise, which they believed could be used to mask a preemptive nuclear strike by NATO against the Soviet Union, that they loaded nuclear warheads onto bombers, bringing NATO and the Soviet Union to the brink of a nuclear war.

Later, upon receiving intelligence reports about the Soviet fear of a U.S. preemptive nuclear strike, President Ronald Reagan commented that,

> We [the U.S.] had many contingency plans for responding to a nuclear attack. But everything would happen so fast that I wondered how much planning or reason could be applied in such a crisis…six minutes to decide how to respond to a blip on a radar scope and decide whether to unleash Armageddon! How could anyone apply reason at a time like that?

This revelation led to a change in attitude on the part of a president who, until then, was known for labeling the Soviet Union as the

"Evil Empire" and joking about launching nuclear missiles against the Soviet target.

A little more than four years after ABLE ARCHER '83, Reagan sat down with Soviet General Secretary Mikhail Gorbachev and signed the Intermediate Nuclear Forces Treaty, a landmark agreement which, for the first time in arms-control history, eliminated an entire class of nuclear weapons from the arsenals of both the U.S. and Soviet Union.

One can only hope that the current nuclear crisis will result in a similar arms control breakthrough in the not-so-distant future.

[This article was originally published in *Consortium News*, October 19, 2022.]

CHAPTER EIGHTEEN
The Hobson's Choice

Russia experts and national security specialists will be poring over the text of Russian President Vladimir Putin's address on Tuesday for some time to come, trying to divine hidden meaning.

The fact is, however, Putin's speech was something rarely heard in Western political circles—unvarnished statements of fact, set forth in a straightforward, surprisingly easy-to-understand manner.

In a world where Western politicians regularly dissemble to shape perception, even if the underlying "facts" are not true (one need only refer to President Joe Biden's infamous phone call with former Afghan President Ashraf Ghani, in July 2021, for an example), Putin's speech was a breath of fresh air—no hidden agendas, no false pretense—no lies.

And on the issue of arms control, the truth hurts.

"I have to say today," Putin announced near the end of his address, "that Russia is suspending its participation in New START. I repeat, not withdrawing from the treaty, no, but merely suspending its participation."

The New Strategic Arms Reduction Treaty (New START), signed in 2010 as the outcome of negotiations between U.S. President Barack Obama and Russian President Dmitry Medvedev, ostensibly caps the number of strategic nuclear warheads that each country can deploy at 1,550; limits the number of deployed land- and submarine-based missiles and bombers used to deliver these warheads to 700; and caps at 800 the deployed and non-deployed ICBM launchers, SLBM launchers and heavy bombers equipped for nuclear armaments.

In February 2021, Biden and Putin agreed to extend the treaty for an additional five years. New START will expire in 2026.

The backstory to New START is important, especially in the context of Putin's declaration regarding Russia's suspension. The core of that backstory is missile defense.

In December 2001, then-President George W. Bush announced that the United States was withdrawing from the landmark 1972 anti-ballistic missile (ABM) treaty, which banned (with limited exception) the development and deployment of missile defense systems designed to shoot down intercontinental ballistic missiles (ICBMs).

The ABM treaty set in stone the Cold War concept of mutually assured destruction, or MAD, the idea that no side possessing nuclear weapons would use them against another nuclear power for the simple reason that to do so would bring about their own demise through guaranteed nuclear retaliation.

The insanity of MAD helped pave the way for all arms control agreements that followed, from the Strategic Arms Limitation Treaty (SALT), to the Intermediate-Range Nuclear Forces (INF) treaty and on to the various iterations of Strategic Arms Reduction treaties (START).

Putin condemned the U.S. decision to withdraw from the ABM treaty as "a mistake." At the time, U.S. and Russian strategic nuclear arsenals were subject to the limitations imposed by the 1991 START treaty. Efforts to further reduce U.S. and Russian nuclear weapons were undertaken as part of the START II treaty.

But post-Cold War politics, combined with the U.S. decision to abandon the ABM treaty, left the treaty signed but unratified, effectively killing it.

Similar issues helped conspire to kill the START III treaty in the negotiation stage. The narrowly focused Strategic Offensive Reductions Treaty, or SORT, which was signed in 2002, committed both the U.S. and Russia to additional reductions beyond those mandated by START I, but contained no verification or compliance mechanisms.

The START I treaty expired in 2009, and SORT in 2012. New START was intended to replace both agreements.

One of the sticking points has been the issue of missile defense. Under President Putin, Russia refused to enter any new substantive arms control treaty (SORT was more informal agreement than treaty in structure and substance) that did not meaningfully address missile defense.

But in May 2008, Dmitry Medvedev took over as Russian president. The Russian constitution prohibited a president from serving more than two consecutive terms in office, and so, with Putin's support, Medvedev ran for Russia's highest office and won. Putin was subsequently appointed prime minister.

While the Bush administration sought to negotiate a follow-on treaty to the soon-to-be expired START I, Medvedev proved to be every bit as reluctant to entering any agreement with the U.S. that did not include limitations on missile defense, something President Bush would not accept.

In the end, the problem of negotiating a new treaty would be left to the administration of Barack Obama, who assumed office in January 2009.

In their first meeting in London in late March 2009, the two leaders issued a statement in which they agreed "to pursue new and verifiable reductions in our strategic offensive arsenals in a step-by-step process, beginning by replacing the Strategic Arms Reduction Treaty with a new, legally binding treaty."

As for missile defense, Obama and Medvedev agreed to treat it as a separate issue. "While acknowledging that differences remain over the purposes of deployment of missile defense assets in Europe," the statement read, "we discussed new possibilities for mutual international cooperation in the field of missile defense, taking into account joint assessments of missile challenges and threats, aimed at enhancing the security of our countries, and that of our allies and partners."

Let there be no doubt—the New START treaty that was negotiated between Russia and the United States, while singularly focused on reducing strategic offensive nuclear arsenals, contained a clear understanding that this treaty would be followed by a good-faith effort by the U.S. to address Russia's longstanding concerns over missile defense.

This was reflected in the exchange of non-binding unilateral statements attached to the New START treaty. The "Statement of the Russian Federation Concerning Missile Defense" set out the position that New START "may be effective and viable only in conditions where there is no qualitative or quantitative build-up in [U.S. missile defense system capabilities]."

Moreover, the statement said any build-up in U.S. missile defense capabilities which gave "rise to a threat to [Russia's strategic nuclear force potential]" would be considered one of the "extraordinary events" mentioned in Article XIV of the treaty and could prompt Russia to exercise its right of withdrawal.

For its part, the United States issued its own statement declaring that U.S. missile defenses "are not intended to affect the strategic balance with Russia" while declaring that it intended "to continue improving and deploying its missile defense systems in order to defend itself against limited attack."

The agreements reached between Obama and Medvedev, however, were not necessarily acceptable to Putin. According to Rose Gottemoeller, the U.S. negotiator for New START, Putin, as prime minister, nearly scuttled the talks when, in December 2009, he once again raised the issue of missile defense.

Chapter Eighteen: *The Hobson's Choice*

"They [the Russians] were going to have a critical National Security Council meeting," Gottemoeller later recounted in an October 2021 talk with the Carnegie Council, "and the story I have heard told is that Putin, for the first time showing some interest in these negotiations, walks into the National Security Council meeting and simply draws lines through all the issues on this decision sheet and said, 'No, no, no, no, no.'"

Gottemoeller went on to describe how Putin then travelled to Vladivostok and delivered a speech where he denounced the treaty as "totally inadequate," criticizing both the U.S. and Russian negotiating teams as being "only focused on limiting strategic offensive forces," noting that "they are not limiting missile defense. This treaty is a waste of time," Gottemoeller quoted Putin. "We should get out of the negotiations."

According to Gottemoeller, Medvedev stood up to Putin, telling his prime minister, "No, we are going to continue these negotiations and get them done."

Anatoly Antonov was the Russian negotiator for New START. He dutifully complied with his instructions from the Kremlin to craft a treaty focused on the reduction of strategic offensive weapons, working under the assumption that the U.S. would be as good as its word when it came to engaging in meaningful negotiations on missile defense.

And yet, less than a year after New START entered into force, Antonov found that the U.S. had no intention on following through on its promises.

In an interview with *Kommersant* newspaper, Antonov said that talks with NATO on a planned Western European missile-defense system had reached "a dead end," adding that NATO proposals were "vague" and that the promised participation of Russia in the proposed system "is not even up for discussion."

Antonov indicated that the lack of good faith shown by the U.S. regarding missile defense could lead to Russia withdrawing from the New START treaty altogether.

While the U.S. did offer to let Russia observe specific aspects of a specific test of a U.S. missile interceptor, the offer never amounted to anything, with the U.S. downplaying the abilities of the SM-3 missile when it came to intercepting Russian missiles, noting that the missile lacked the range to be effective against Russian missiles.

The late Ellen Tauscher, who at the time was the U.S. undersecretary of state for arms control and international security, had offered Antonov written assurances that the Mark 41 Aegis Ashore system, which would employ the SM-3 missile interceptor, was not directed against Russia.

However, Tauscher said, "We cannot provide legally binding commitments, nor can we agree to limitations on missile defense, which must necessarily keep pace with the evolution of the threat."

Tauscher's words were prophetic. In 2015, the U.S. began testing the SM-3 Block IIA interceptor against ICBM targets. The SM-3 did, in fact, have the range to shoot down Russian intermediate- and intercontinental-range missiles.

And now those interceptor missiles were to be stationed on bases constructed in Poland and Romania, two former Warsaw Pact nations that were closer to the border with Russia than NATO forces had ever been.

The Americans had negotiated in bad faith. Putin, it turned out, had been right to question a strategic arms control treaty that did not consider Russia's concerns over missile defense.

And yet this did not weaken Putin's commitment to fulfilling New START. According to Gottemoeller, "Putin, since this treaty has been signed, has taken a very positive stance about it. Since the treaty has entered into force, he has called it repeatedly publicly the 'gold standard' of nuclear treaties and has supported it...I know that he has been committed to the treaty and really committed to the efforts underway now in this strategic stability dialogue to get some new negotiations going."

But Putin's assiduous adherence to New START did not mean that the Russian leader had stopped worrying about the threat posed by U.S. missile defense. On March 1, 2018, Putin delivered a major address to the Russian Federal Assembly—the same forum he spoke to on Tuesday. His tone was defiant: "I want to tell all those who have fueled the arms race over the last 15 years, sought to win unilateral advantages over Russia, and introduced unlawful sanctions aimed at containing our country's development—everything that you wanted to impede with your policies has already happened. You have failed to contain Russia."

Putin then unveiled several new Russian strategic weapons, including the Sarmat heavy ICBM and the Avangard hypersonic vehicle, which he said were developed in direct response to the U.S. withdrawal from the ABM treaty.

Putin said Russia had warned the U.S. that it would take such measures back in 2004. "No one listened to us then," Putin declared. "So listen to us now."

One of the people listening was Rose Gottemoeller. "[P]eople are worried about ... the new so-called exotic weapons systems that President Putin rolled out in March of 2018," the former arms control negotiator, by then retired, said in 2021. "[T]wo of them are already under the limits New START, the so-called Sarmat heavy [ICBM] and also the Avangard, which is their first strategic-range hypersonic glide vehicle that they are getting ready to deploy. They have already said that they will bring it under the New START Treaty."

Gottemoeller noted that any future arms control agreement would be seeking constraints on these systems.

The New START Treaty was extended for a five-year term in February 2021, even though the Russians believed that the "conversion or elimination" procedures used by the U.S. to determine whether B-52H bombers and Ohio-class submarines converted from nuclear- to non-nuclear use, or eliminated altogether, were insufficient.

The Russians hoped that these issues could be worked out using the treaty-mandated Bilateral Consultative Commission (BCC) process, which meets twice a year to resolve issues such as these.

One of the problems facing both the U.S. and Russian inspectors and negotiators, however, was the Covid-19 pandemic. In early 2020, both sides agreed to suspend on-site inspections and BCC meetings due to the pandemic. By mid-2021, U.S. and Russian negotiators began discussing the creation of joint Covid protocols that could get both inspections and BCC consultations up and running.

But then came Ukraine.

On March 9, 2022, the U.S., U.K. and European Union all passed sanctions which banned Russian aircraft from overflying their respective territories and placed visa restrictions on Russians transiting EU or the U.K. enroute to the United States. According to the Russians, these restrictions effectively prohibit the dispatch of weapons-inspection teams to the U.S. using New START short-notice inspection protocols, which have strict treaty-mandated timelines attached to their implementation.

In June 2022, the U.S. unilaterally declared that the moratorium on inspections imposed because of the Covid-19 pandemic was no longer in effect. On August 8, 2022, the U.S. attempted to dispatch a short-notice inspection team to Russia to carry out treaty-mandated inspection tasks.

Russia denied entry to the team and accused the U.S. of trying to gain a unilateral advantage by conducting on-site inspections while Russia could not. Citing the restrictions imposed by sanctions, the

Chapter Eighteen: *The Hobson's Choice*

Russia Foreign Ministry said, "there are no similar obstacles to the arrival of American inspectors in Russia."

To resolve the impasse over inspections as well as other outstanding treaty-implementation issues, Russian and U.S. diplomats began consultations on convening a meeting of the BCC, and eventually were able to settle on a November 29, 2022, date in Cairo, Egypt. Four days before the BCC was supposed to begin, however, Russia announced that the meeting was off.

Russian Deputy Foreign Minister Sergei Ryabkov, in statements made to *Kommersant*, said that the war in Ukraine was at the heart of the decision. "There is, of course, the effect of what is happening in Ukraine and around it," Ryabkov said. "I will not deny it. Arms control and dialogue in this area cannot be immune to what is around it."

The State Department issued an official report to Congress on Russian compliance with New START in early 2023 which accused Russia of violating the New START treaty by refusing U.S. inspectors access to sites inside Russia.

Russia, a State Department spokesperson stated, was "not complying with its obligation under the New START Treaty to facilitate inspection activities on its territory," noting that "Russia's refusal to facilitate inspection activities prevents the United States from exercising important rights under the treaty and threatens the viability of U.S.-Russian nuclear arms control."

The insensitivity of the U.S. side to the impact of its actions targeting Russia—sometimes literally—as part of the overall U.S. response to Putin's initiation of the Special Military Operation in February 2022 is, however, telling.

In his address on Tuesday, Putin highlighted the role played by the U.S. and NATO in facilitating the Ukrainian use of Soviet-era drones to carry out an attack on a base near Engels, Russia, that housed Russia's strategic aviation assets, including nuclear-capable bombers. He also pointed out that he had just signed orders for the Sarmat and Avangard systems to become operational and, as such, inspectable under the terms of New START.

"The United States and NATO are directly saying that their goal is to inflict a strategic defeat on Russia," Putin said. "Are they going to inspect our defense facilities, including the newest ones, as if nothing had happened? Do they really think we're easily going to let them in there just like that?"

Rose Gottemoeller observed that the U.S. is "not going to change our policy on Ukraine because he's [Putin] in a hissy fit over the New START treaty. That's just not going to happen."

But Putin's stance is far more principled than a simple "hissy fit." Born of the original sin perpetrated by the U.S. in withdrawing from the ABM treaty, Putin's angst is directly tied to the deceit displayed by U.S. officials—including Gottemoeller—when it came to assurances given Dmitry Medvedev about missile defense during the New START negotiations.

This deceit led to Russia deploying new categories of strategic nuclear weapons—the Sarmat and Avangard—to defeat U.S. missile defense systems, including those that had been forward deployed into Europe.

And now, with the war in Ukraine being linked to a U.S. strategy of achieving the strategic defeat of Russia, the U.S. is seeking to use New START to gain access to these very systems, all the while denying Russia its reciprocal rights of inspection under the treaty. As Putin aptly noted, such an arrangement "really sounds absurd."

The inability and/or unwillingness of either party to compromise on New START means that the treaty will remain in limbo for the indefinite future which, given that the treaty expires in February 2026, means there is a distinct possibility arms control between the U.S. and Russia is dead.

Chapter Eighteen: *The Hobson's Choice*

While the U.S. and Russia had previously committed to a follow-on treaty to replace New START, the ongoing conflict between Russia and Ukraine poses a nearly insurmountable obstacle for anyone seeking to have such a treaty document ready for signature and ratification by the time New START expires.

There is a good chance the U.S. and Russia, in two years' time, will find themselves without any verifiable mechanism to assuage the fears and uncertainty about the two parties' respective nuclear arsenals, leading to the real possibility—if not probability—that they will both embark on an unconstrained arms race fueled by ignorance-based angst that could very well result in the kind of misunderstandings, mistakes, or miscalculations that could trigger a nuclear war and, in doing so, end all humanity.

"The truth is behind us," Putin said, closing out his address to the Russian Federal Assembly.

So, too, may be humanity's last chance to prevent nuclear calamity, if a way can't somehow be found to get arms control back on the agenda.

Here, Gottemoeller's assertion that the U.S. would not alter its Ukraine policy to save New START underscores the self-defeating reality of the Biden administration's efforts to arm Ukraine.

The sooner the war in Ukraine is over, the sooner the U.S. and Russia can get down to the business of preserving arms control as a viable part of the relationship between the two nations.

By seeking to extend the Ukraine conflict, however, the U.S. is in effect engaging in an act of self-immolation that threatens to engulf the world in a nuclear holocaust.

During the Vietnam War, the noted correspondent Peter Arnett quoted an unnamed U.S. Army officer as saying, "We had to destroy the village to save it." With regard to the linkage that has been created between Ukraine and arms control, the same sick logic now applies—to save one, the other must be destroyed.

To save Ukraine, arms control must be destroyed.

To save arms control, Ukraine must be destroyed.

One sacrifices a nation, the other a planet.

This is the Hobson's Choice U.S. policy makers have created, except it is not.

Save the planet. That is the only choice.

[This article was originally published in *Consortium News*, February 23, 2023.]

CHAPTER NINETEEN
Lowering the Threshold

Russia's decision to deploy nuclear weapons on Belarusian soil is the latest in a series of escalatory moves by both the U.S. and Russia that erodes the viability of arms control agreements going forward and, in doing so, increases the possibility of nuclear conflict between them.

Russian President Vladimir Putin recently announced that Russia will deploy tactical nuclear weapons to Belarus. This decision was ostensibly in response to a request by Belarusian President Alexander Lukashenko and is framed as a reaction to U.S. and NATO statements that both Putin and Lukashenko construe as constituting a policy that seeks the strategic defeat of Russia and, by extension, Belarus.

The nuclear weapons—which would involve warheads for the Iskander-M short-range, surface-to-surface missile, as well as gravity bombs delivered by Belarusian SU-30 aircraft—would remain under Russian control and would only be turned over to Belarus if a joint decision was made to deploy nuclear weapons against any emerging threat to Belarus. According to Russian media reports, Russia has already transferred both the Iskander-M missiles and launchers and the SU-30 fighters to the Belarusian armed forces, who have been trained in the use of nuclear weapons. The actual transfer of nuclear weapons, however, would occur only in July 2023, when a planned nuclear storage facility would be completed on Belarusian soil.

The Russian decision to deploy nuclear weapons to Belarus, and to make them available to Belarusian forces in time of conflict or crisis, has a precedent—a decades-long program of nuclear sharing between the U.S. and NATO, whereby the U.S. stores 100 B61 nuclear bombs at U.S.-controlled facilities in the Netherlands, Belgium, Germany,

Italy and Turkey. The bombs are considered to be U.S. property, but in the event of hostilities, the U.S. would release them to the air forces of six NATO allies (the five hosts plus Greece). These possess aircraft configured for the use of nuclear weapons, flown by crews trained for that task. In response to the war in Ukraine, Poland has asked to become a party to this nuclear-sharing arrangement.

The release of U.S.-controlled B61 bombs to NATO air forces is practiced every year, in an exercise known as Steadfast Noon. The 2022 iteration of this event took place from October 17–30 and involved 60 aircraft from 14 nations flying simulated nuclear strike missions over Belgium, the U.K. and the North Sea. The exercises included U.S. B-52 aircraft, whose nuclear capacity is treated as separate from the NATO nuclear deterrent from an arms control perspective. Russia, however, contends that the two are, for all intents and purposes, inseparable, with the presence of nuclear-capable B-52 bombers in the Steadfast Noon exercise highlighting the interoperability between the U.S. and NATO-designated nuclear arsenals.

While advocates of arms control have long argued that the B61 bombs are obsolete and should be negotiated away as part of any future arms control agreement between the U.S. and Russia, NATO has argued that its nuclear deterrent is necessary to ensure that the notion of a U.S. nuclear umbrella over Europe is sustained by a discernable link between the U.S. and NATO nuclear deterrence forces. Although the administration of President Barack Obama considered removing the B61 bombs from Europe, this idea was shelved following the Russian annexation of Crimea in 2014.

The linkage between the B61 bombs and the overall U.S. nuclear posture becomes more critical, from the Russian perspective, when considering that the U.S. nuclear posture under the administration of President Joe Biden articulates that the "fundamental role" of the U.S. nuclear arsenal is deterrence from a nuclear attack, whereby nuclear

Chapter Nineteen: *Lowering the Threshold*

weapons could be used in "extreme circumstances to defend the vital interests of the U.S. or its allies and partners," including pre-emptively in a non-nuclear scenario. This posture deviates from Biden's campaign pledge to implement a "sole purpose" doctrine built on the premise that the "sole purpose of the U.S. nuclear arsenal should be deterring—and, if necessary, retaliating against—a nuclear attack."

The Biden administration instead opted to continue with a nuclear posture tied to principles dating to the administration of President George W. Bush and delineated in the 2020 Nuclear Posture Review published by the administration of President Donald Trump. The deputy undersecretary of defense for policy during the Trump administration, David J. Trachtenberg, said in a speech at the Brookings Institution in 2019 that U.S. allies and partners "should and do take comfort in the fact that the U.S. has both the will and the means to use its nuclear weapons, if necessary, to protect them from aggression," adding that a key aspect to the U.S. nuclear posture was "keeping adversaries such as Russia and China guessing whether the U.S. would ever employ its nuclear weapons." To accomplish this, Trachtenberg noted, the Trump administration, along with previous administrations, "refused to countenance the promise to not use nuclear weapons as a first-strike option."

From the Russian perspective, the continuation of this policy of not ruling out the possibility of a U.S. nuclear first strike positions the B61-equipped NATO nuclear deterrent as an existential threat that justifies a Russian-Belarusian nuclear counter—and, equally importantly, requires a fundamental rethinking of Russia's relationship with arms control and nuclear disarmament going forward. The U.S. posture has become critical for Moscow in light of U.S.-NATO statements regarding the strategic defeat of Russia in Ukraine.

Russia recently announced that it had frozen implementation of the New START nuclear arms reduction treaty, blaming the inconsistencies of seeking to negotiate further restrictions of Russia's strategic deterrent with a party—the U.S.—that it sees as pursuing the strategic defeat of Russia in Ukraine.

Central to the Russian point of view is the idea that, as a nuclear power, Russia cannot be defeated—because to accomplish this, any opponent would need to pose the kind of existential threat that would trigger the use of nuclear weapons. Russia sees nuclear deterrence as its lifeline, and to negotiate this away in the face of such a threat is unthinkable for Moscow.

The Biden administration has rejected Moscow's concerns as unfounded and considers the Russian suspension of New START as an impermissible act under the treaty terms. While the U.S. maintains that it is prepared to discuss all relevant issues with Russia to bring New START back into operation, and that it is prepared to begin working with Russia on a follow-on disarmament treaty to replace the treaty when it expires in February 2026, U.S. officials see no linkage between U.S. policy on Ukraine and strategic arms control—and as such refuse to participate in any process that sustains such an assumption.

Further complicating matters is the fact that, according to Russian diplomatic and military sources, Moscow has also changed the ground rules regarding any future negotiations. The U.S. should now add the B61 bombs to the mix of weapons that would need to be covered by any future arms control agreement, Moscow believes. Washington should no longer be able to delink missile defense issues from nuclear force reductions. And the nuclear forces of both France and the U.K., once deemed outside the context of bilateral U.S.-Russian arms control, should be incorporated into the force structure when considering any possible future Russian reductions or limitations, Moscow believes.

Seen in this context, the Russian decision to extend its nuclear umbrella to Belarus is a game-changing event, which has fundamentally altered the trajectory of arms control between the world's two

Chapter Nineteen: *Lowering the Threshold*

largest nuclear powers. It remains to be seen how the U.S. and NATO will respond to this new dynamic—or if they will opt instead to engage in a new and dangerous arms race with Russia, the consequences of which could be detrimental for all humanity.

• • •

In an appearance at the plenary session of the Valdai Discussion Club on October 5, 2023, Russian President Vladimir Putin announced that Russia had successfully tested the Burevestnik "nuclear-powered global-range cruise missile."

This effectively brought to fruition a journey he had announced back in a speech delivered on March 1, 2018, when he unveiled a series of new Russian strategic weapons designed as a response to America's continued nullification of arms control agreements regarding missile defense.

In his 2008 address, Putin had outlined the efforts undertaken by Russia over the years to get the U.S. to scale back missile defense programs Russia viewed as representing an existential threat to its survival. "You didn't listen to our country then," Putin concluded. "Listen to us now."

Chief among Russia's concerns was that continued U.S. pursuit of missile defense capabilities, when coupled with an American nuclear posture that envisioned the possibility of pre-emptive nuclear war, could create the conditions in which U.S. nuclear war planners could believe that an American first strike designed to neutralize Russia's strategic nuclear capability, when combined with a missile defense shield the U.S. believed could shoot down most, if not all, of any Russian missiles that might survive such an attack, might actually be viable.

In the audience at the Valdai Discussion Club was Sergey Karaganov, a well-known Russian political scientist who, in an article titled "A Difficult but Necessary Decision," published on June 13, 2023, in the journal *Russia in Global Affairs,* articulated in favor of Russia moving away from a nuclear posture based upon assured nuclear retaliation to one that favored pre-emption. "We will have to make nuclear deterrence a convincing argument again," Karaganov wrote, "by lowering the threshold for the use of nuclear weapons set unacceptably high, and by rapidly but prudently moving up the deterrence-escalation ladder."

According to Karaganov, "If we correctly build a strategy of intimidation and deterrence and even use of nuclear weapons, the risk of a 'retaliatory' nuclear or any other strike on our territory can be reduced to an absolute minimum. Only a madman," Karaganov argued, "who, above all, hates America, will have the guts to strike back in 'defense' of Europeans, thus putting his own country at risk and sacrificing conditional Boston for conditional Poznan."

If such a madman did, in fact exist, then, Karaganov noted, "we will have to hit a bunch of targets in a number of countries in order to bring those who have lost their mind to reason. Morally, this is a terrible choice as we will use God's weapon, thus dooming ourselves to grave spiritual losses. But if we do not do this, not only Russia can die, but most likely the entire human civilization will cease to exist."

President Putin, using the prerogative that is accrued through his position, called on Karaganov to ask a question. This was no accident, given the outcry that had followed the publication of Karaganov's article, which led to much speculation that Putin was considering adopting a nuclear posture along the lines proposed by Karaganov. The Russan academic did not disappoint, asking the Russian President whether it was not time for Russia to change its approach to nuclear arms and restore its deterrent strength in the eyes of Western elites who repeat endlessly that Russia is weak.

Chapter Nineteen: *Lowering the Threshold*

It was a trap. "I have read your article," Putin responded, before laying out a detailed answer that made it clear to all who listened that the Russian president did not agree with Karaganov's thesis. "From the moment the launch of missiles is detected," Putin said, "no matter where it comes from—from any point of the world ocean or from any territory—such a number, so many hundreds of our missiles appear in the air in a retaliatory strike that there is no chance of survival, there will be no single enemy left, and in several directions at once." Putin urged America to understand that any threats against Russia are "absolutely unacceptable for any potential aggressor."

In short, President Putin was reinvigorating the Cold War-era nuclear posture of mutually assured destruction as Russia's go-to nuclear doctrine.

Moreover, Putin noted, Russia would launch a nuclear attack against any country or countries that threaten its continued existence as a sovereign state, regardless of whether the threat posed is by nuclear arms or conventional arms. Since there is no such existential threat to Russia today, the Russian President concluded, there is no reason to threaten the use of nuclear arms.

However, Putin said, there was one aspect of Russian nuclear policy that could, and indeed should, be changed—Russia's ratification of the Nuclear Test Ban Treaty. The United States, Putin noted, had signed the treaty, but had never ratified it. Given Russia's modernization of its nuclear arsenal, which included, in addition to the Burevestnik cruise missile, the Sarmat heavy intercontinental ballistic missile, the Poseidon nuclear torpedo, and hypersonic delivery vehicles, many in the Russian military were demanding that Russia resume nuclear testing to be sure that the new cutting-edge strategic weapons systems that constitute the heart of Russia's strategic nuclear forces perform as intended.

Putin observed that this very same question had been discussed in the United States by its military officials, who were, de jure, unrestrained by a treaty that had not been ratified, and as such never entered into force.

Thus, the big news out of the Valdai Discussion Club isn't a new Russian missile or nuclear posture. The big news is that the Russian president will be sending a bill to the Russian Duma that would revoke Russia's ratification of the test ban treaty. Russia won't be the first to resume testing of nuclear weapons. But if the United States were to go down that path, then Russia would respond immediately. The important point here is that any U.S. testing would be done in support of either legacy nuclear weapons that are in dire need of being replaced, or future nuclear weapons which have yet to be developed and fielded.

Russia, as Putin underscored, has already modernized its nuclear force. If the United States were to resume a nuclear arms race by returning to nuclear testing, Russia would begin such a race with an insurmountable lead in nuclear delivery systems.

Game, set, match—Russia.

[This chapter is comprised of two articles: "The Future of U.S.-Russia Nuclear Arms Control," published in *Energy Intelligence*, April 11, 2023, and "Russia Throws Down the Nuclear Gauntlet," published in *Sputnik*, September 10, 2023.]

CHAPTER TWENTY
The Growing Threat of Nuclear War

The United States finds itself wandering in a wilderness of indecision when it comes to arms control policy.

The situation regarding the status of the last existing nuclear arms control treaty with Russia— the New START treaty—is dire. Implementation is currently frozen after Russia suspended its participation in protest to a stated U.S. policy objective of seeking the strategic defeat of Russia, something Russia finds incompatible with opening its strategic nuclear deterrent (which exists precisely to prevent Russia's strategic defeat) to inspection by U.S. officials.

The U.S. is not talking with Russia about the future of arms control once New START expires in February 2026.

Moreover, fallout from the U.S. policy of seeking strategic defeat of Russia has seen Moscow radically alter its position regarding future arms control treaties. Any future agreement must, from the Russian perspective, include missile defense; the French and British nuclear arsenals, as well as the U.S.-supplied NATO nuclear deterrent.

Russia has further complicated any future negotiations by deploying tactical nuclear weapons to its Baltic enclave in Kaliningrad, as well as extending its Russian-controlled nuclear umbrella to Belarus where it has mirrored the NATO nuclear umbrella.

The state of play today regarding strategic arms control between the U.S. and Russia can best be likened to a patient on life support whom no one is trying to revive.

Russia is in the process of finalizing a major modernization of its strategic nuclear forces, built around the new Sarmat heavy intercontinental ballistic missile (ICBM) and the Avangard hypersonic reentry vehicle. The United States is on the cusp of initiating its own multi-billion-dollar upgrade to the U.S. nuclear triad consisting of the B-21 stealth bomber, the Columbia class missile submarine and the new Sentinel ICBM.

If no treaty vehicle exists designed to verifiably limit the deployment of these new weapons, once New START expires, the U.S. and Russia will find themselves engaged in an unconstrained nuclear arms race that dramatically increases the probability of unintended nuclear conflict.

When viewed in this light, the future of global security hinges on the ability of Russia and the U.S. to return to the negotiating table and resuscitate arms control from its present moribund state.

Key to this will be the willingness of Washington to incorporate Russian concerns into U.S. nuclear posture. To achieve this, the U.S. nuclear establishment will have to be shaken out of the calcified policy assumptions that have guided U.S. arms control policy since the end of the Cold War.

First and foremost, amongst these assumptions is the need to promote and sustain U.S. primacy in global nuclear weapons capability. Whether such an assumption is jettisoned will be tied to the person occupying the White House after the February 2026 expiration of New START.

This makes the 2024 U.S. presidential election one of the most critical in recent history. Simply put, the future of humanity may ride on whomever the American people vote for in November 2024.

President Joe Biden has indicated that he will be seeking a second term in office. While some have opined that, given Biden's age, this goal might be too optimistic, the reality is that if Biden, Vice President Kamala Harris, or some other person designated by the Democratic Party is in office to continue the Biden administration's agenda for

Chapter Twenty: *The Growing Threat of Nuclear War*

another four years, decisions on the future of the U.S. nuclear posture and, by extension, arms control policy, will remain in the hands of the same establishment that has put us in the situation we are in today.

It's proper to ask, therefore, whether or not the "establishment" is capable of implementing the changes necessary to get U.S.-Russian arms control back on track. History suggests not.

Biden ran in 2020 on a promise to change U.S. nuclear strategy away from the George W. Bush–era policy, when preemptive U.S. nuclear strikes were a possibility, to a doctrine holding that U.S. nuclear forces exist for the sole purpose of deterring a nuclear attack against the U.S. or retaliating if deterrence failed.

However, once elected, Biden's promise fell to the wayside as an "interagency process" run by unelected bureaucrats and military officers intervened to prevent campaign rhetoric from becoming official policy.

Biden, like every American president before him in the nuclear age, has been unable and/or unwilling to expend the political capital necessary to take on the American nuclear enterprise, and as a result the American people and the rest of humanity are held hostage by this deadly nexus between the U.S. military industrial complex and the U.S. Congress.

Congress allocates taxpayer money to underwrite a nuclear weapons–oriented defense industry, which in turn feeds this money back into campaign contributions that empower a compromised Congress to keep funding the nuclear enterprise—creating a vicious cycle impervious to change of its own volition.

Biden or anyone Democratic candidate in 2024 is a byproduct of this very establishment, and a willing participant in the corrupt circle of money and power that is the nuclear, military-industrial-congressional complex. In short, if Biden or his proxy is sitting in the White

House in 2025, there will be no change in the U.S. nuclear posture on arms control policy.

This means any Democratic Party–controlled candidate voted into office in November 2024 may very well be the last president to hold office, given the probability of nuclear war between the U.S. and Russia, which an unchanged nuclear posture and arms control policy will foster.

Donald Trump, who preceded Biden as the occupant of 1600 Pennsylvania Avenue, has thrown his hat into the 2024 presidential race.

Given the current state of the Republican Party, which has been cowed into submission to Trump's "make America great again" brand of populist politics, it's highly unlikely the GOP will put up a primary candidate capable of defeating Trump, his ongoing legal dramas notwithstanding.

Whether Trump could pull off a second successful presidential run is not the issue here. Instead, the question is whether Trump can promote an arms control stance different from Biden and the Democratic and Republican establishments that could break free of existing constraints—giving arms control a chance.

Trump's track record is decidedly mixed in this regard. On the one hand, he has articulated some foundational beliefs which, if incorporated into official U.S. policy, could radically alter the way the U.S. relates with the rest of the world and, in doing so, create a new paradigm capable of sustaining a revised arms control policy.

Trump's willingness to break free of the ideological prison of rampant Russophobia by considering the possibility of friendly relations between the U.S. and Russia makes him unique among mainstream presidential candidates of either party.

Likewise, Trump's questioning of NATO's viability and purpose means that a future Trump administration could engage in the kinds of policy restructuring that ends the perpetual state of tension between NATO and Russia since NATO needs a Russian threat to justify its existence.

NATO'S diminishment as a policy driver would free both the U.S. and Europe to more rationally explore the potential for a new European security framework in a post–Ukraine conflict world. Such a posture would, in one fell swoop, help resolve many of the add-on issues Russia now insists must be part of any future U.S.-Russian arms control agreement, including missile defense, French and U.K. nuclear weapons and the U.S.-provided NATO nuclear deterrent.

More important, however, is Trump's proven track record in breaking free of past policy precedent in pursuit of meaningful nuclear disarmament.

The case of North Korea stands out. Trump met with North Korean leader Kim Jong Un on three separate occasions to try to bring about the denuclearization of North Korea. While ultimately this gambit failed, in large part because of the resistance to change on the part of establishment figures like Trump's secretary of state, Mike Pompeo, and National Security Advisor John Bolton, the fact that Trump even went down that path shows that, unlike his predecessors and successor, he was willing to go the extra mile in pursuit of ground-breaking change in U.S. arms control policy.

But there is another side to Trump which bodes poorly for any meaningful change in U.S.-Russian arms control. First and foremost is his abysmal record on arms control.

He withdrew from the Iran nuclear deal, he withdrew from the Intermediate Nuclear Forces treaty and he published as policy the most aggressive nuclear posture document in recent history, one which, according to Trump officials, was designed to "keep the Russians guessing" as to whether the U.S. would preemptively use nuclear weapons.

Trump refused to meaningfully engage with the Russians on any aspect of arms control, and instead embraced the modernization of U.S. strategic nuclear forces. In short, there was no light between Trump's arms control policy and that of the "establishment." Indeed, one might make the case that Trump's policies represented an escalation over the norm.

Then there is Trump's tendency toward pugilistic bluster driven, apparently, by some inner insecurity that requires any U.S. negotiating position to be taken from a posture of overwhelming strength and dominance. He spoke of being "friends" with Russia, only to openly brag about being the "toughest president ever" when it came to sanctioning Russia.

He withdrew from the Iran nuclear agreement, imposing new sanctions, all the while promoting the idea of a new negotiation that would resolve the Iran nuclear issue. And his North Korean initiative included some of the most war-like rhetoric uttered by an American president in the nuclear age, promising "fire and fury" if North Korea failed to toe the line.

The bottom line is that the "Trump Standard" for arms control is in many ways even more dangerous than that of the "establishment," promoting as it does an aggressive posture founded in dominance.

In the end, Trump proved incapable of acting on his own belief, allowing himself to be subordinated to a radical America-first national security ideology which promoted the enhancement and expansion of the American nuclear enterprise—the exact opposite trajectory the U.S. needs to be taking come 2024.

There is no reasonable expectation that a second Trump term would deviate meaningfully from that track record.

The harsh reality today is that neither of the two potential sources of viable presidential candidates for the 2024 election—Democratic National Committee or MAGA Republicans—are positioned to effect

Chapter Twenty: *The Growing Threat of Nuclear War*

meaningful, positive change regarding either U.S. nuclear posture or underlying arms control policy.

That leaves the American people, and the world as a whole, with the inevitability of a massive nuclear arms race between the U.S. and Russia, which will unfold unconstrained by meaningful arms control treaty-mandated limitations.

This is nothing short of a recipe for disaster, a witch's brew of ignorance-based fear magnified by the lack of inspections designed to mollify concerns over the respective nuclear threats posed by two nations no longer willing to engage in meaningful dialogue and, as a result, perched on the precipice of an apocalyptic abyss.

In short, a vote for either Biden/the Democratic establishment or Trump/MAGA Republicans is a vote in favor of continuous nuclear-armed Russian roulette, where there exists only one certainty—eventually the pistol will go off. But in this case, it's not a pistol, but a nuclear weapon that leads to general nuclear war and the termination of life on planet earth as we currently know and understand it.

The rally held in Washington, D.C., on February 19, 2023, provided a platform for some voices of sanity who have presidential potential, either as independent candidates, or rogue outliers within their respective party establishments. Tulsi Gabbard, Dennis Kucinich, Ron Paul, and Jimmy Dore all addressed the threat posed by nuclear weapons and the need to control them through meaningful arms control.

But none who spoke have put anything in writing that would remotely constitute an arms control "standard" that could compete with either Biden or Trump—or their proxies—on the public stage. Moreover, other than Dore, a comedian, none of these individuals has announced an intention to run, making moot, for the moment at least, the notion of a third option on arms control and American nuclear posture.

Robert F. Kennedy, Jr., the nephew of former President John F. Kennedy, has announced his intention to challenge Biden for the Democratic nomination. While Kennedy, at this juncture, appears to be a long shot, the likely mental and physical deterioration and possible incapacitation of Biden between now and November 2024, combined with the inadequacy of Vice President Kamala Harris as a presidential candidate, means the Democratic field could be thrown open.

Kennedy's announcement puts him in a position to be either the candidate himself, or to challenge whatever establishment figure the Democratic Party selects for the job.

The question is whether Kennedy is willing or able to articulate a new American standard on arms control, one that embraces the best of the Trump Standard without the pugilistic arrogance Trump brings with it.

Kennedy has not published a detailed position on arms control and the U.S. nuclear posture. But in a recent conversation with me, he spoke about the legacy of his uncle, Jack Kennedy, and how he took guidance from that legacy.

Any man who draws upon the wisdom and patience displayed by President Kennedy to defuse the Cuban Missile Crisis would be on the right track when it comes to arms control.

•••

In the background of the political, military and economic machinations around the ongoing Russian-Ukrainian conflict is the ever-present threat of nuclear war. Many pundits and policymakers in the West see this threat as overblown, believing, for example, that Russia is bluffing when it speaks of implementing its nuclear doctrine in response to NATO intervention in Ukraine. But the threat of nuclear war is real and growing.

Chapter Twenty: *The Growing Threat of Nuclear War*

The world faces a greater threat of a nuclear conflict between the U.S. and Russia than at any time since the Cuban Missile Crisis of 1962. In many ways, the present danger is more acute, given that the mechanisms of diplomacy that helped prevent war then are not engaged today. Moreover, in October 1962, the nuclear arms race had not yet reached full stride—the weapons possessed by the two nuclear-armed adversaries then pale in quantity, quality and lethality to the arsenals that exist today.

And while the size of the present-day arsenals has been significantly reduced from the height of the Cold War, the institutional "muscle memory" that exists in both the U.S. and Russia from that time makes the rapid rearmament of nuclear arsenals possible when the restrictions imposed by the last remaining arms control treaty—the 2010 New START treaty—expire on February 4, 2026. Indeed, the U.S. has already spoken of nuclear rearmament "without restrictions" once the treaty's caps are lifted.

In its 2010 Nuclear Posture Review, the administration of President Barack Obama de-emphasized the role of nuclear weapons in U.S. security strategy by narrowing nuclear contingencies to the deterrence of an enemy nuclear attack. It moved away from the more expansive posture promulgated in the 2002 Nuclear Posture published by the administration of George W. Bush, which allowed for the preemptive use of nuclear weapons in a non-nuclear scenario. But the 2018 Nuclear Posture Review conducted under then-President Donald Trump returned to the Bush-era policy, allowing the potential use of the U.S. nuclear arsenal to deter "significant non-nuclear strategic attacks."

In 2020, then-presidential candidate Joe Biden declared that, if elected, he would implement a policy where deterring a nuclear attack should again be the sole purpose of the U.S. nuclear arsenal. However, the Biden administration's 2022 Nuclear Posture Review remained largely unchanged from Trump's 2018 version.

This means, in effect, that the U.S. today has a nuclear policy that incorporates scenarios where new "low-yield" nuclear warheads on Trident submarine-launched ballistic missiles could be used preemptively to enforce deterrence models predicated on the notion of "escalate to deescalate." Put simply, the U.S. could use nuclear weapons to compel an adversary or enemy to back down from actions that do not involve the use of nuclear weapons. The U.S. has emphasized its forward-leaning nuclear posture in reassuring its allies—especially in NATO—that the U.S. nuclear umbrella is viable in times of crisis.

The conflict between Russia and Ukraine, which has evolved into a de facto proxy conflict between NATO and Russia, has raised the specter of direct nuclear confrontation between the trans-Atlantic alliance and the Russian Federation for the first time since the Cold War. NATO has placed increased emphasis on the role of nuclear weapons in any potential conflict scenario involving Russia and recently discussed the possibility of placing up to 24 U.S.-supplied B-61 bombs on operational status, meaning they could be loaded onto specially designated NATO aircraft for use at a moment's notice. This would make any launch of nuclear-designated aircraft equivalent to a potential nuclear attack in the mind of the Russian government.

Russian nuclear doctrine has remained largely consistent since it was first publicly declared in 2010. Under this, Moscow reserves the right to use nuclear weapons not just in response to the use of nuclear weapons or other types of weapons of mass destruction against Russia or its allies, but also in the event of aggression with conventional forces that threatens the existential survival of Russia.

The threshold appeared to be lowered after Russia's invasion of Ukraine in February 2022, when Moscow linked its nuclear arsenal to potential Russian reactions to U.S. and NATO interventions. Since then, the situation has devolved further, with the U.S. and NATO embracing a policy posture that seeks the "strategic defeat" of Russia in Ukraine. Currently, the parameters for such a defeat include evicting Russia from five Ukrainian territories it has annexed. Russia has rejected any effort by the U.S. to engage in nuclear arms control talks so long as the official policy of the U.S. is its strategic defeat.

Russia has responded to changes in the U.S. nuclear posture over the years by modernizing its strategic nuclear forces and by extending its nuclear umbrella to Belarus, where it has implemented a nuclear weapon-sharing program. Moscow believes that the Biden administration's decision to leave the 2018 Nuclear Posture unchanged, combined with the potential NATO decision to place 24 B-61 bombs on operational status, lowers the U.S. threshold for the use of nuclear weapons. Russia reacted by announcing in June 2024 that it would undertake a review of its own nuclear posture to see if it, too, needed to lower its threshold. Moscow followed this announcement with full-scale drills of its tactical nuclear forces in Belarus in early July 2024.

The danger of a world without arms control agreements is manifest. One need only look at the impact of the U.S.'s 2018 decision to withdraw from the 1987 Intermediate Nuclear Forces (INF) treaty, a landmark agreement that eliminated the most destabilizing class of nuclear weapons in the world at that time from the U.S. and Soviet/Russian arsenals—missiles with a range of between 500 and 5,500 kilometers. The U.S., together with Germany, recently announced it would begin redeploying intermediate-range missiles to Europe in 2026. In response, Russia declared that it would resume production of intermediate-range missiles and match the U.S. deployment with its own.

The re-emergence in Europe of weapons previously banned under the now-defunct INF treaty would not simply re-impose the existential threat that these weapons represented when initially deployed in the 1980s but expand it exponentially. The new intermediate-range systems will include hypersonic missiles that, given their speed and accuracy, virtually ensure the destruction of their target within minutes of being launched. The first-strike potential of these weapons means that an adversary must have their own retaliation capability ready for a hair-trigger response.

The potential deployment of nuclear-armed cruise and hypersonic missiles by the U.S. in Europe in 2026, combined with Russia's likely response, effectively subordinates the existing protocols for the use of U.S. strategic nuclear weapons to European contingencies. Russian President Vladimir Putin recently declared that since the new intermediate-range missiles will threaten Russia's strategic command and control infrastructure, there is no difference from the Russian perspective between a European conflict and a U.S.-Russian conflict.

Current protocols regarding the release of nuclear weapons by both sides envisage a 15- to 30-minute deliberation period for executive review, consultation and approval of any nuclear weapons release. However, in a future scenario involving European-based hypersonic missiles, the time between launch and impact of a U.S. hypersonic intermediate-range missile would be less than 10 minutes. The time available for deliberation would be reduced to less than six minutes—leaving no time for protocol-based executive coordination and consideration of options.

In short, the deployment of intermediate-range missiles in Europe would put both sides in a position where any suspected missile launch would be treated as real upon detection, and thus trigger an immediate retaliatory strike.

As things stand, come 2026, any mistake, miscalculation or misjudgment by either the U.S., NATO or Russia could—and most likely would—prompt preemption by the other party. While nuclear planners in the U.S. believe there are scenarios in which a limited

Chapter Twenty: *The Growing Threat of Nuclear War*

nuclear conflict could be limited to Europe, Russian nuclear doctrine holds that any use of nuclear weapons against Russian territory will be responded to with a general nuclear attack using the totality of its strategic nuclear arsenal. As such, any scenario involving the threat of a European-based nuclear first strike against Russia could escalate quickly into a general nuclear exchange—in short, a global annihilation event.

[This chapter is comprised of two articles: "The Future of U.S. Nuclear Strategy," published in *Consortium News*, April 7, 2023, and "The Growing Threat of Nuclear War," published in *Energy Intelligence*, July 30, 2024.]

CONCLUSION
F*ck Them/72 Hours

Russian President Vladimir Putin is known for a lot of things—his "in your face" speeches, his marathon unscripted press conferences and his stoic impassiveness in the face of adversity come to mind.

One thing that doesn't jump out at the average observer is his earthy sense of humor. Long-time Putin watchers know that the Russian leader on occasion spices up his formal presentations with off-color quips which, unless one is well versed in colloquial Russian of the back-alley variety, can get missed by the casual listener.

During the June 16 discussion period of the plenary session of the 2023 St. Petersburg International Economic Forum, the Russian leader was asked about his views on the potential use of nuclear weapons in the context of the ongoing Ukrainian conflict.

"This use of nuclear weapons is certainly theoretically possible," Putin bluntly answered.

"For Russia, this is possible if a threat is created to our territorial integrity, independence and sovereignty, the existence of the Russian state. Nuclear weapons are created in order to ensure our security in the broadest sense of the word and the existence of the Russian state."

Putin's answer reflected long-standing Russian nuclear doctrine, which postulates the use of nuclear weapons in the case of an existential threat, nuclear or otherwise, to the survival of Russia.

Putin then sought to put the audience at ease. "But we, firstly, do not have such a need," Putin noted, "and secondly, the very factor of reasoning on this topic already lowers the possibility of lowering the threshold for the use of weapons. This is the first part."

What came next was classic Putin. "The second is that we have more such weapons [i.e., tactical nuclear weapons] than the NATO

Conclusion: F*ck Them/72 Hours

countries. They know about it and all the time they persuade us to start talks on reductions."

Putin paused, before shrugging and, with a half-smile, saying "*Khren Im.*"

Khren Im is a Russian slang term derived from the word "horseradish" (*khren*), thus a literal translation of the phrase used by Putin would be "horseradish them." But *khren* closely resembles a saltier term used to describe male genitalia, and when used in this manner, *khren Im* is understood to mean "F*ck them."

"F*ck them, you know?" Putin said, to the obvious mirth of the audience. "As our people say. Because, in the clumsy terms of economics, this is our competitive advantage."

The "them" in the horseradish reference made by the Russian president is the United States. Two weeks prior to Putin's man-in-the-street reaction, on June 2, U.S. President Joe Biden's national security adviser, Jake Sullivan, addressed a conference hosted by the Arms Control Association, in Washington, D.C. The topic, not surprisingly, was the administration's approach to U.S.-Russian arms control.

Sullivan made it clear to his audience that the nuclear strategy that the Biden administration approved in October 2022 would remain intact through 2026, when the last remaining U.S.-Russian arms control agreement, the 2010 New START treaty, was set to expire.

Once the New START treaty expires and barring any agreement replacing it with a new agreement, Sullivan said that, given the state of play between the U.S. and Russia when it came to arms control, the U.S. would have no choice but to develop and deploy newer, more dangerous nuclear weapons.

Sullivan then laid out the Biden administration's case against Russia, starting with the Russian suspension of the New START treaty itself. Left unsaid was Russia's stated reason for this suspension, namely the impossibility from the Russian point of view of engaging in strategic nuclear arms reductions at a time when the United States was pursuing a policy in Ukraine of waging a proxy conflict designed to cause the strategic defeat of Russia.

From the Russian perspective, pursuing the cooperative reduction with the U.S. of the very strategic capability which is, by design, intended to prevent Russia's strategic defeat at a time when the U.S. was pursuing the strategic defeat of Russia was a non-starter.

Likewise left unspoken was Russia's contention that the U.S. was in violation of the New START Treaty by keeping some 101 strategic delivery systems from being inspected, despite being required to do so by the provisions of the New START Treaty.

Khren Im.

Sullivan called out Russia's decision to station tactical nuclear weapons in Belarus, without elaborating on either the threats made to Belarus by several NATO members, including Poland and the Baltic states. Nor did he acknowledge that the Russian action parallels a similar U.S. policy in stationing some 100 nuclear B-61 gravity bombs on the territories of five NATO nations.

Khren Im.

Sullivan strongly criticized Russia for its total disregard for international law, including arms control treaties such as the Treaty on Conventional Forces in Europe (CFE) from which Russia recently withdrew, without putting the Russian decision in proper historical perspective.

This perspective involves the ongoing disregard by the U.S. and NATO of deliberate inequities in the CFE structure that were brought on by the ongoing expansion of NATO. Nor did the U.S. national security adviser acknowledge that it was the U.S., not Russia, which had withdrawn from the Anti-Ballistic Missile Treaty and the Intermediate Forces Treaty, both of which are considered foundational for all arms control treaties going forward.

Khren Im.

Sullivan's presentation ignored such salient matters as the purpose behind NATO's certification of the F-35 fighter as a nuclear-capable delivery system, and what the deployment of nuclear-capable F-35s to NATO nations not included in the existing shared nuclear defense scheme meant to the scope and scale of the NATO nuclear deterrence model considering the continued NATO Baltic Air Policing and South European Air Policing operations.

Sullivan also failed to address the current "launch-on-warning" posture employed by the Biden administration, which positions the U.S. to carry out a first nuclear strike against Russia, and the role that the continued patrols in Europe and Asia by American nuclear-capable B-52H strategic bombers, including aggressive flight profiles appearing to simulate the launch of nuclear-armed cruise missiles against Saint Petersburg.

Sullivan also ignored the impact of the Biden administration's ongoing plans to bring back medium- and intermediate-range nuclear-capable missiles to the European theater will have on the overall nuclear balance of power between the U.S.-NATO and Russia.

Khren Im.

A day before Putin addressed the St. Petersburg International Economic Forum, Russian Deputy Foreign Minister Sergei Ryabkov spoke to the media about the "opposing, irreconcilable positions" of Russia and the U.S. concerning the resumption of discussions regarding the New START treaty. "[T]he suspension of New START remains in effect," Ryabkov said, "and this decision may be revoked or reconsidered only if the U.S. demonstrates a willingness to abandon its fundamentally hostile policy toward the Russian Federation."

Khren Im.

Neither Putin nor Ryabkov seemed to be concerned about Jake Sullivan's rhetorical posturing before the Arms Control Association.

The same cannot be said for Sergey Karaganov, a noted Russian political scientist, economist and academic. On June 13, Karaganov published an article, "A Difficult but Necessary Decision," in the journal *Russia in Global Affairs*. In it, Karaganov praises nuclear weapons as "God's weapon" and calls for Russia to launch a nuclear strike on "a bunch of targets in a number of countries in order to bring those who have lost their mind to reason."

Karaganov argues that, in response to the policies of the U.S.-led collective West which seek the strategic defeat of Russia, and because, in his opinion, Russia lacks the conventional military capacity to achieve anything more than a "frozen" conflict in Ukraine that would condemn it to a state of perpetual conflict with Ukraine and the collective West, Russia must "build a strategy of intimidation and deterrence and even use of nuclear weapons" which, if done correctly, would result in "the risk of a 'retaliatory' nuclear or any other strike on our territory can be reduced to an absolute minimum."

"Only a madman," Karaganov notes, "who, above all, hates America, will have the guts to strike back in 'defense' of Europeans, thus putting his own country at risk and sacrificing conditional Boston for conditional Poznan. Both the U.S. and Europe," Karaganov concludes, "know this very well, but they just prefer not to think about it."

Biden seems to be leaning toward a similar conclusion. At a fundraiser where he denounced Russia's decision to station tactical nuclear weapons in Belarus, Biden spoke about his fear that Putin may resort to the use of tactical nuclear weapons.

"When I was out here about two years ago saying I worried about the Colorado River drying up, everybody looked at me like I was crazy," Biden said. "They looked at me like when I said I worry about Putin using tactical nuclear weapons. It's real," Biden concluded.

It's real.

Conclusion: *F*ck Them/72 Hours*

No kidding, Mr. President. It is as real as it gets. While people are right to be concerned about the policy recommendations made by prominent Russians such as Karaganov, they must also address the root cause of such pronouncements, namely the policies of the Biden administration to achieve the strategic defeat of Russia in Ukraine, seemingly at whatever cost (especially when the cost is paid in the blood of Ukrainian soldiers).

Russia will not use nuclear weapons to fulfil the tasks set forth in its Special Military Operation. It will use nuclear weapons to preserve Russian territorial integrity.

The reality today is, thanks to the irresponsible policies of the U.S. and its NATO allies, who have sought the expansion of NATO up to the Russian borders while foregoing every opportunity to prevent a conflict with Russia over Ukraine, there is a war between Russia and Ukraine that has resulted in Ukraine irrevocably losing 20 percent of its territory (the oblasts of Kherson, Zaparizhia, Donetsk and Lugansk, along with the Crimea).

All of that territory has been absorbed into the Russian Federation and makes any effort to strip them away from Russia by definition an existential conflict where, if Russia were to lose, would necessarily trigger the use of nuclear weapons.

And yet Biden and his NATO allies continue to feed a Ukrainian fantasy where the reacquisition of these territories by Ukraine is a desirable outcome.

Has either Biden, his advisers, or the American public considered the potential consequences of this action? Are they willing to trade Boston for Poznan, or sacrifice humanity for the sake of appeasing Ukrainian sensibilities?

The answer appears to be "no."

As for Russia, one is guided by the words of Vladimir Putin: "*Khren Im*"

F*ck them.

But, in reality, F*ck us.

All of us.

If this insanity is allowed to continue unabated, it is lights out for all of humanity.

Chew on that the next time you cheer on the Ukrainian counteroffensive or applaud the use of U.S. taxpayer dollars to fund the Ukrainian military.

It is high time for the American public to recognize that our only hope for a survivable future is one where arms control and nuclear disarmament once again serve as the cornerstone of a U.S.-Russian relationship, and that the shortest possible path toward achieving that objective is for Russia to win its war against Ukraine.

And for those politicians in the U.S. and Europe who have invested their political futures on the suicidal mission of feeding Ukraine's anti-Russian fantasies?

Khren Im.

• • •

Most Americans approached last weekend thinking about how they would spend the much-anticipated end of the work week with their friends and family.

Few realize how close they came to actualizing the scenario so horrifyingly spelled out in Annie Jacobsen's alarming must-read book, *Nuclear War: A Scenario.*

72 minutes.

That is all it takes to end the world as we know it.

That is less time than most movies playing at the local cinema.

Most people could not drive to the local home improvement store to buy the materials needed to do the little repairs around the home that usually wait for the weekend.

Conclusion: F*ck Them/72 Hours

Walk the dogs?

Play with the kids?

Forget about it.

72 minutes.

And everything you thought you lived your life for would be dead.

And if you survived?

To quote Nikita Khrushchev, "The survivors would envy the dead."

Ukraine, together with many of its NATO allies, has been asking for permission from the United States, the United Kingdom, and France to be able to employ precision-guided long-range weapons systems provided by these countries against targets deep inside Russia.

On September 6, at a meeting of the Ramstein Contact Group, a forum where U.S.-NATO military support to Ukraine is coordinated, Ukrainian President Volodymyr Zelensky personally appealed to the group for more weapons support from its Western allies and called on allies to allow Ukraine to use the weapons they provided to strike deeper inside Russia.

"We need to have this long-range capability," Zelensky said, addressing the attendees, who included U.S. Secretary of Defense Lloyd Austin, "not only on the divided territory of Ukraine but also on Russian territory so that Russia is motivated to seek peace. We need to make Russian cities, and even Russian soldiers think about what they need: peace or Putin."

Secretary Austin, in comments made afterwards, said he didn't think the use of long-range missiles to strike inside Russia would help end the war, adding that he expected the conflict would be resolved through negotiations. Moreover, Austin noted, Ukraine had its own weapons capable of attacking targets well beyond the range of the British Storm Shadow cruise missile.

Despite Austin's pushback, President Joe Biden appeared to be on track to give Zelensky the green light he was looking for regarding the use of British-provided Storm Shadow cruise missiles and U.S.-provided long-range ATACMS (Army Tactical Missile System) missiles for strikes on Russian soil.

On September 11, U.S. Secretary of State Antony Blinken, accompanied by British Foreign Secretary David Lammy, visited Ukraine, where they held meetings with Zelensky and his newly appointed foreign minister, Andrii Sybiha.

Blinken and Lammy, however, failed to make the announcement the Ukrainians were waiting with bated breath to hear. Instead, Blinken and Lammy reiterated the full support of their respective nations to Ukraine's victory, adding that they would adapt their support to meet Ukrainian needs. "The bottom line is this: We want Ukraine to win," Blinken said after his meeting with Zelensky.

The stage was now set for Keir Starmer, the prime minister of the United Kingdom, to fly to Washington, DC, last Friday, where he would meet with Biden and jointly agree to give Ukraine permission to use Storm Shadow and ATACMS against targets inside Russia.

Russia has long made it clear that it would view any nation which authorized the use of its weapons to strike Russia as a direct party to the conflict.

In comments to the media in Russia last Thursday—one day before the Biden-Starmer meeting at the White House—Russian President Vladimir Putin made it clear that any lifting of the restrictions on Ukrainian use of U.S.- and U.K.-provided long-range weapons would change "the very essence of the conflict." He said: "This will mean that NATO countries, the United States, European countries are fighting Russia. And if this is the case, then…we will make appropriate decisions in response to the threats that will be posed to us."

Kremlin spokesperson Dmitry Peskov, speaking after Putin's announcement, noted that the Russian president's words were "extremely clear" and that they had reached their intended audience—U.S. President Biden.

Biden didn't seem happy about the message. In responding to a question from reporters prior to his meeting with Prime Minister Starmer at the White House about what he thought about Putin's warning, Biden snapped angrily, "I don't think much about Vladimir Putin."

The evidence suggests otherwise.

At a White House press conference that same day, Robbie Gramer, the White House correspondent for *Politico*, asked John Kirby, the spokesperson for the National Security Council, "Do you take Putin at his words that strikes into Russian territory by U.S.—or British—or French-made missiles would actually expand the war?"

Kirby's response was telling in many ways. "It's hard to take anything coming out of Putin's face at his word. But this is not rhetoric that we haven't heard from him before, so there's really not a lot new there."

Gramer followed up: "So, in other words, you know, in the deliberations about this long-range strike, threats from Putin are not a big factor for you guys in your deliberations on this?"

"Well," Kirby responded, "you didn't let me finish the answer, so let me try…I never said, nor have I—would we ever say that we don't take Mr. Putin's threats seriously. When he starts brandishing the nuclear sword, for instance, yeah, we take that seriously, and we constantly monitor that kind of activity. He obviously has proven capable of aggression.

He has obviously proven capable of escalation over the last, now, going on three years. So, yeah, we take these comments seriously, but it is not something that we haven't heard before. So, we take note of it. Got it. We have our own calculus for what we decide to provide to Ukraine and what not. And I think I'd leave it there."

Just to drive the point home, Russia's ambassador to the United Nations, Vassily Nebenzia, told the Security Council last Friday that NATO would "be a direct party to hostilities against a nuclear power," if it allowed Ukraine to use longer range weapons against Russia. "You shouldn't forget about this and think about the consequences," he declared.

The finishing touches on driving home the seriousness of Putin's warning was left to the Russian ambassador to the United States, Anatoly Antonov. Speaking to the Russian media also last Friday Antonov said he was surprised that many American officials believed that "if there is a conflict, it will not spread to the territory of the United States of America. I am constantly trying to convey to them one thesis that the Americans will not be able to sit it out behind the waters of this ocean. This war will affect everyone, so we constantly say—do not play with this rhetoric."

Putin's words had caught the attention of several former U.S. government officials, who had called Antonov for clarification.

"Yesterday's statements from Vladimir Putin were weighed very carefully here. Several ex-officials called me asking to explain what actually stands behind those statements. I simply replied: 'Don't play with fire.'"

Antonov's sentiments were likely to echo through existing back-channel communications used by the Department of Defense and the C.I.A.

In the end, the message got through—Biden pulled back from giving Ukraine the permissions it sought.

Most Americans are unaware about how close they came to waking up Saturday morning, only to find that it was their last.

Had Biden yielded to Starmer's pressure (the British, together with Ukraine and several NATO nations, believed that Putin was bluffing), and signed off on the permission, Ukraine was prepared to launch strikes on Russia that night.

(British soldiers deployed in Ukraine would be needed to operate the Storm Shadows and they are already there, according to German Chancellor Olaf Scholz, who has refused to send similar weapons to Ukraine.)

Russia would likely have responded with conventional attacks on Kiev using new weapons, such as the Avangard hypersonic warhead, which would each deliver a blow equivalent to 26–28 tons of explosives.

Russia would also most likely have struck NATO targets in Poland and Romania where Ukrainian fighters are based. And, lastly, Russia would have struck British military targets, possibly including those on the British Isles.

This would prompt a NATO retaliation under Article 5, using a large number of NATO long-range strike weapons targeting Russian command and control, airfields, and ammunition storage facilities.

The Russian response would most likely involve the launching of more Avangard conventional warheads against NATO targets, including Ramstein airbase and NATO headquarters, as well as airbases from which strikes against Russia were launched.

At this juncture the United States, using nuclear employment plans derived from a nuclear posture which emphasizes the pre-emptive use of low-yield nuclear weapons to "escalate to deescalate"—i.e., force Russia to back down through a demonstration of capability—would authorize the use of one or more low-yield nuclear warheads against Russian targets on Russian soil.

But Russian doctrine has no capacity for engaging in a limited nuclear war. Instead, Russia would respond with a general nuclear retaliation targeting all of Europe and the United States.

Whatever U.S. strategic forces that survived this onslaught would be fired at Russia.

And then we all die.

72 minutes.

And the world ends.

We were one stroke of the pen away from this outcome on Friday, September 13, 2024.

This isn't a drill.

This isn't an academic exercise.

This is the real world.

This is life or death.

This is your future held hostage by a madman in Kiev, backed by lunatics in Europe.

The question is—*what are we going to do about it?*

There is an election on November 5 where the next commander-in-chief of the United States will be selected by "we, the people."

This person will be the one holding the pen in any future scenario where life or death decisions that could manifest into a general nuclear war will be made.

It is incumbent upon we, the people, to make sure that Americans demand the candidates for this office articulate their policy vision regarding the war in Ukraine, the prospects of peace with Russia, and what they will do to prevent the outbreak of nuclear war.

But they won't do that if we, the people, remain silent about the issue.

Stand up. Speak out. Demand to be heard.

72 minutes is all it takes to end life as we know it.

We almost all died over the weekend of September 14–15, 2024.

Conclusion: *F*ck Them/72 Hours*

What are we going to do to make sure that doesn't happen again?

[This chapter is a combination of two articles published in *Consortium News,* on June 21, 2023, and September 19, 2024.]

INDEX

3M14 Kalibr sea-launched cruise missile 37, 45, 67

A
ABLE ARCHER '83 151, 152
Aegis-equipped navy vessels 129
Afghanistan 7, 21, 54
Alas, Babylon (novel) 19
American Conservative viii, 32, 68, 130
American people 19, 96, 103, 136, 137, 150, 174, 175, 179, 198
Anti-Ballistic Missile (ABM) 10–11, 15, 17, 26, 30, 34–35, 37, 50, 53, 70, 72, 81, 98, 154, 159
Anti-Ballistic Missile (ABM) Treaty xiv, 7, 11, 17, 18, 26, 30, 34, 37, 50, 53, 60, 70, 78, 154, 162, 188
Antonov, Anatoly 157, 158, 196
AN/TPY-2 X-band radar 129
Armageddon iii, vii–viii, xxi, 146, 148–149, 151
Arms Control Association 187, 189
Army Tactical Missile System (ATACMS) 194
Arnett, Peter 163
Asia 61, 70, 72, 92, 189
al-Assad, Bashar 122
Austin, Lloyd 193–194
Australia 145
Avangard hypersonic nuclear weapons systems 80, 104, 159, 162, 174, 197

B
B-2 bomber 80
B-21 stealth bomber 80, 174
B-52 bomber 12, 81, 149, 166
B-52H heavy bomber 36–37, 78, 99, 160, 189
B-61 nuclear bomb xxv, 81, 149, 165–168, 182–183, 188
Ballistic Missile Defense (BMD) 17
ballistic-missile submarines 13
Baltics 7, 20, 21, 149, 173, 188–189
Belarus 165, 167–168, 173, 183, 188, 190
Belgium 165–166
Ben-Gurion, David 139
Ben Gvir, Itamar 138
Biden, Joe xxi, xxii, xxiii, xxv, xxvi, 8, 77, 79–82, 95–98, 101, 115, 146–147, 148, 150, 153, 163, 166–168, 174–176, 179–183, 187, 189–191, 194–197
Bilateral Consultative Commission (BCC) 99–101, 160–161
Billingslea, Marshall 89–96, 103, 107
Blinken, Antony 77, 98, 101, 194
Bolton, John 34, 59, 60, 63, 72, 177
Boston Globe viii
"breakout time" 131–133
Bronson, Rachel 48
Brookings Institution 167
Bulletin of the Atomic Scientists 48, 49, 58
Burevestnik nuclear missile 169, 171
Bush, George W. xvi, 11, 26, 34, 60, 72, 98, 133, 148, 154–155, 167, 175, 181

C
Carlucci, Frank xv
Carnegie Council 157

Index

Carnegie Endowment for International Peace xxi
Carnegie-Tsinghua Center for Global Policy 117
Carter, Jimmy 6
Cartwright, James 3
Cheney, Richard xvi
China v, xiv, xxi, xxiii, xxiv, xxv, xxvi, 5, 50, 53, 59, 60–61, 72–73, 82–83, 85–86, 89–90, 103, 107, 109, 111–127, 167
  2006 Defense White Paper 111–112, 114
  nuclear arsenal xxiv, 115
  nuclear capabilities 60
  nuclear umbrella 124
  State Council Information Office 111
Chinese People's Liberation Army Rocket Force 112
CIA 196
  Arms Control Intelligence Staff (ACIS) 64, 65, 66
  Nonproliferation Center (NPC) 64, 65
Cirincione, Joseph 54
Clinton, Bill 11, 26, 48, 65, 72
Clinton, Hillary 24
Coats, Dan 38, 66, 67
Cold War xiv, xv, xxii, 4, 7, 8, 11, 14, 26, 28, 50, 52, 59, 69–70, 72, 78, 103–104, 107, 116, 119, 122, 154, 171, 174, 181–182
Colorado 83
Colorado River 190
Columbia class submarine 80, 174
Comprehensive Test Ban Treaty 50
Consortium News viii, xxvi, 152, 164, 185, 199
Conventional Forces in Europe (CFE) treaty 78, 188
Cost Assessment and Program Evaluation (CAPE) 106
Council for a Livable World xxii

Countryman, Thomas 54
covert conditioning 140
Covid-19 pandemic 82, 99, 103, 160
Crimea 20, 56, 166, 191
Cuban Missile Crisis of 1962 57, 70, 71, 98, 102, 146, 150, 180, 181

D

Democrats 8, 95, 97, 174–176, 178–180
DF-5 missile 112–113
DF-26 missile 72
DF-31 missile 113–114
DF-41 missile 113–115, 117
Dimona nuclear weapons production facility xvii, 139–140
Doomsday Clock 48–50, 58
Dore, Jimmy 179
Dr. Strangelove xv

E

Eisenhower, Dwight D. xiii, 70, 121
Eliyahu, Amichai 138
Ellsberg, Dan xiii
Energy Intelligence viii, 47, 73, 107, 130, 141, 172, 185
Estonia 7
Europe v, 6, 7, 11, 43–47, 53, 56–58, 61, 62, 69, 70–73, 77, 81, 118, 120, 145, 149, 155, 162, 166, 177, 183–185, 188–190, 192, 198
European Union 160

F

F-35 fighter 189
Foreign Affairs xxii
"forward-based systems" 70

France 50, 111, 116, 139, 140, 168, 177, 193
Frank, Pat 19

G

Gabbard, Tulsi 179
Gaddafi, Muammar 122
"game theory" 6
Gaza xiv, xv, 138
Geneva Summit (June 2021) 79
Georgia xvi, 20, 22
Germany 44, 57, 165, 183
Ghani, Ashraf 153
Glitman, Maynard 52, 54
Global Zero Commission 3
Gorbachev, Mikhail 6, 25, 52, 61, 63, 70, 104, 152
Gottemoeller, Rose 156, 157, 158, 159, 162, 163
Graham, Thomas Jr. 51, 64–65, 68
Gramer, Robbie 195
Greece 166
Ground Based Strategic Deterrent (GBSD) 82, 83, 84, 85, 86, 106
ground-launched cruise missile (GLCM) 37, 38, 39, 45, 51, 118
  9M728 38, 56, 67
  9M729 37–38, 44–45, 53, 55–56, 66–67

H

Haldeman, Bob 148
Hamas 137–141
hardened missile silos 83
Harris, Kamala 174, 180
Hart, Alan xviii, xix
Helms, Jesse 52
Helsinki Summit 69
Heritage Foundation 92, 95
Hezbollah 137, 141
Hiroshima 30, 69, 138
Hobson's Choice v, 6, 153, 164
Ho Chi Minh 148

Hudson Institute 103
Huffington Post viii, 15
Hussein, Saddam 122
Hutchinson, Kay Bailey 43
Hu Xijin 117
Hwasong-16B hypersonic missile 126–127
Hwasong-18 hypersonic missile 127
hydrogen bomb 49
hypersonic delivery vehicles 171
hypersonic weapons 9–10, 12, 14, 31, 34, 80, 104, 126–129, 159, 171, 174, 184, 197

I

India 50, 53, 60, 116, 124
inter-agency xxiii
intercontinental ballistic missile (ICBM) 3–4, 9–11, 13–15, 31, 35–36, 72, 77, 80, 82–88, 91, 104–107, 112–117, 119, 126, 153–154, 158–159, 174, 184
Intermediate-Range Nuclear Forces (INF) 52, 61–63, 73, 118, 120
Intermediate-Range Nuclear Forces (INF) Treaty v, xv, xvi, xxiii, 11, 25–26, 37–73, 78, 81, 89, 98, 113–114, 118, 152, 154, 177, 183, 188
  INF talks 52
International Atomic Energy Agency (IAEA) 131, 133–134
International Economic Forum (St. Petersburg, 2023) 186, 189
Iran v, 5, 11, 46–47, 50, 64, 66, 68, 109, 129, 131–141, 177–178
Iraq 11, 21, 54, 64–66, 68, 122, 133, 136
Iskander-M missiles 165
Israel v, xi, xvii–xviii, 109, 116, 129, 131, 133, 135, 137–141
  Israel Defense Forces 141
Italy 166

Index

J
Jacobsen, Annie 192
Japan xii, 9, 30, 121, 123, 124, 126, 128, 129, 138
Jeremiah xi, xiii
Jilantai training area 113, 114
Joint Comprehensive Program of Action (JCPOA) 131–137
Jupiter missiles 57

K
Kang Sok-Ju xvi
Karaganov, Sergey 169, 170, 171, 190, 191
Kelly, Jim xvii
Kennedy, John F. 6, 70, 139, 150, 180
Kennedy, Robert F., Jr. 180
Kerry, John 20
Kh-101 air-launched cruise missile 37
Khren Im 187–192
Khrushchev, Nikita 150, 193
Kiev 197, 198
Kim Jong-il xvi
Kim Jong Un 149, 177
Kirby, John 195
Kohler, Foy 150
Kommersant (newspaper) 89, 157, 161
Korean armistice agreement 121
Korean Peninsula 121, 125, 129, 149
Korean War 49
Kosovo 7
Kucinich, Dennis 179
Kurds 19
Kvitinsky, Yuliy 52

L
Lammy, David 194
Latvia 7
launch-on-warning posture 114
Lavrov, Sergei 13, 15, 56–57, 79, 93–94, 96
Lee Gun xvi
Libya 7, 122, 140
Lithuania 7
Los Angeles Times viii
Lowy Institute 145
Lukashenko, Alexander 165
Lungscu, Oana 145

M
Machon, Annie 57
"Madman Theory" 148
Makeyev JSC 105
Malraux, André xi
Manhattan Project xiii
Marcarelli, Paul 16, 19
Mark 41 "Aegis Ashore" vertical launch system 38–39, 45–47, 63, 89, 91, 158
Mattis, James 14, 29, 32, 44
McChrystal Group Leadership Institute 54
McChrystal, Stanley 54
Medvedev, Dmitry 153, 155–157, 162
Meir, Golda xviii, xix
Middle East 43, 46, 47, 69, 131, 139
Minuteman missiles 3, 4, 5, 62, 80, 86, 105
  Minuteman III 3, 4, 5, 80–88, 105, 116
Mizin, Viktor 50, 51, 54
Montana 3, 83
"Morning Joe" (MSNBC program) 12, 13
Multiple Independently Targetable Reentry Vehicle (MIRV) xv
mutually assured destruction (MAD) v, xv–xvi, 10, 24–25, 33–34, 71, 86, 120, 126, 128, 154, 171
MX Peacekeeper missile 106

N

Nagasaki 30, 69, 138
National Defense Authorization Act (NDAA) 82
National Defense Strategy (NDS) xxiii
National Security Strategy (NSS) xxiii
Nebenzia, Vassily 196
Nebraska 83
Netanyahu, Benjamin xvii, 135, 138, 141
The Netherlands 149, 165
"new abnormal" 48, 58
The New York Times viii, 28, 29
Nitze, Paul 52, 54, 55
Nixon, Richard 6, 139, 148
non-strategic nuclear weapons 81
North Atlantic Treaty Organization (NATO) xvi, xxiv, xxv, 6, 7, 20, 21, 30, 33, 35, 38, 43–47, 50, 51, 53, 56, 59, 61, 63, 72, 79, 81, 90, 100, 116, 118, 145–147, 149–151, 157–158, 161, 162, 165–167, 169, 173, 176, 177, 180, 182–184, 186, 188–189, 191, 193–194, 196–197
   Nuclear Planning Group 44
   nuclear umbrella 173, 145
North Dakota 3, 83
North Korea v, 5, 11, 50, 109, 116, 121–129, 148–149, 177–178
   ballistic missile production capability 126
Northrop Grumman 106
North Sea 166
Norway 62
Novator 66, 67
nuclear ambiguity 139–140
nuclear-armed bombers 4
nuclear deterrence xxv–xxvi, 3, 8–10, 16, 24, 46, 61–62, 83, 86, 120, 124–125, 140, 166, 168, 170, 189
Nuclear Employment Guidance xxiv, xxvi
nuclear symmetry 118
Nuclear Test Ban Treaty 171–172
nuclear testing 14, 33, 37, 55, 66, 113, 127, 140, 158, 171–172
Nuclear War: A Scenario 192
Nuclear Weapons Employment Planning and Posture Guidance xxiv

O

Obama, Barack xxi, 7–9, 11, 13–14, 26, 50, 53, 56, 72, 77, 95, 98, 133–137, 153, 155–156, 166, 181
"Object 4202" hypersonic warhead v, 3, 9, 10, 12
October 7 138, 140
Ohio-class submarine 80, 160
Olmert, Ehud 140
Open Skies Treaty 78, 81
Operation STEADFAST NOON 145, 151
Oppenheimer, Robert xii
Organization for Security and Co-operation in Europe (OSCE) 79
Otzma Yehudit (Jewish Power) party 138

P

Pakistan 50, 53, 60, 116, 124
Patriot 3 missile interceptor 129
Paul, Ron 179
People's Liberation Army Rocket Force 113
Perle, Richard 51–52
Perry, William 48
Pershing II missile 44, 51, 57, 61, 71, 118
Peskov, Dmitry 60, 79–80, 195
Ploughshares Fund 54

Index

Poland 38–39, 43, 45–47, 63, 81, 158, 166, 188, 197
Politico 87–89, 195
Pompeo, Mike 72, 177
Poseidon nuclear torpedo 171
possible military dimensions (PMD) 134
Postol, Ted xv
Powell, Colin xv, xvi
Putin, Vladimir xiv, 12–14, 16–19, 22–25, 27–29, 31, 34–35, 39, 53, 58–60, 63, 69, 79, 92–97, 101, 146–148, 153–159, 161–163, 165, 169–172, 184, 186–187, 189–191, 193–197
Pyongyang xvi, xvii, 122, 123, 124, 126

R

R-36 heavy ballistic missile 30, 31, 32, 105
Rabinowitch, Eugene 49
Ramstein airbase 197
Ramstein Contact Group 193
RAND 4
Reagan, Ronald xv, 6, 8, 11, 24, 25, 27, 51, 52, 63, 70, 81, 116, 151, 152
Republicans 176
Richard, Charles xxiii
Romania 38, 39, 43, 45–47, 63, 81, 158, 197
Rood, John 149
RS-24 Yars missile 104
RS-26 missile 9, 104
RS-28 missile 9–10, 12, 14, 29–32, 105
RS-56 Bulava missile 105
Rusk, Dean 6
Russia viii–ix, xii, xiv, xvi, xxi–xxv, 3–39, 43–50, 53, 55–73, 77–107, 115–117, 119–120, 124, 127, 140, 145–198
Grom (Thunder) drill 149
meddling in 2016 U.S. presidential election 56
military budget 106
nuclear umbrella 168, 173, 183
Russian Duma 172
Russian Federal Assembly 16, 19, 159, 163
Russian Foreign Ministry 43, 88, 101, 161
Russian military 20–21, 28, 171
Russian Ministry of Defense 38
Special Military Operation 161, 191
Statement of the Russian Federation Concerning Missile Defense 156
strategic nuclear forces 171
Russia in Global Affairs 170, 190
Russian Academy of Missile and Ammunition Sciences 60
Russia Today viii, 81, 86, 97, 107, 116, 120
Ryabkov, Sergei 68, 91, 95, 100, 161, 189

S

Saakashvili, Mikheil xvi
Sarmat heavy intercontinental ballistic missile 29, 31, 80, 86, 105, 159, 162, 171, 173
S-band radar 129
Schmidt, Helmut 44
Scholz, Olaf 197
Security Council of the Russian Federation 93, 95
Sentinel missile 80, 174
service life extension programs (SLEP) 84–86
Sharon, Ariel 139–140
Shoigu, Sergei 147
short-range nuclear missiles 6, 60, 128
Site K 46
Sivkov, Konstantin 60

SM-3 missile 46, 63, 91, 129, 158
SM-3 missile interceptors 129
SM-6 surface-to-air missile 38, 39
"sole purpose policy" 147, 167
South Africa 140
South Korea 121, 123–124, 126–129
Special Verification Commission (SVC) 53
Sputnik viii, 172
SS-20 intermediate-range missiles 25, 44, 51–52, 71, 73, 118
Starmer, Keir 194–195, 197
"Star Wars" anti-missile system 11
stealth bomber 13, 174
Stockholm International Peace Research Institute 140
Stoltenberg, Jens 44, 145
Storm Shadow cruise missile 193, 194, 197
Strategic Arms Limitation Treaty (SALT) 52, 70, 154
Strategic Arms Reduction Treaty (START) 11, 50, 64, 72, 154, 155
  New START v, xiv, xxi,–xxvi, 7, 11, 26, 34–39, 57–58, 72–73, 75, 77, 78, 80, 83, 87, 88–103, 117, 119–120, 153–163, 167, 168, 173, 174, 181, 187–189
  START I 30, 155
  START II 30, 154
  START III 154
Strategic Offensive Reductions Treaty (SORT) 96, 154, 155
SU-30 aircraft 165
submarine-launched ballistic missile (SLBM) 4, 35–36, 72, 77–78, 83–84, 88, 89, 105, 107, 115, 117, 119, 182
  RS-56 Bulava 105
  SLBM launchers 88–89, 153
Sullivan, Jake 187–189
surface-to-surface missile 165

Sybiha, Andrii 194
Syria 8, 19–21, 22, 46, 122, 141

T

Taiwan xxiv
Tauscher, Ellen 158
Tenth Review Conference for the Treaty on the Non-Proliferation of Nuclear Weapons 77
THAAD 125, 129
Thompson, Andrea 54–58, 67–68
Tillerson, Rex 14
The Times of London xix, 13
Tomahawk sea-launched cruise missile 38, 63
TPY-2 radar 46–47
Trachtenberg, David J. 167
Treaty on Conventional Forces in Europe (CFE) 188
Trident ballistic missile submarine 88
Trident D5 system 112, 114
Trident SLBM launcher 36–37, 78, 99
  U.S. conversion of 88–89
Trident submarine-launched ballistic missile (SLBM) xxii, 5, 36, 81, 149
  D-5 87–88
trilateral arms control 119, 120
Trump, Donald xxii–xxiii, 5, 7–8, 12–16, 19, 22–23, 26, 28–29, 37, 48, 50, 54, 56, 58–60, 63, 69, 73, 77, 87, 90, 93–98, 102–103, 119, 122, 131, 133, 135–137, 148–149, 167, 176–182
  2019 State of the Union address 54
Truss, Liz 147
"Trust but Verify" 81
TruthDig viii, 27, 39, 58, 141
Turkey 46–47, 57, 70, 166

Index

U

Ukraine xv, xvi, xxiv, 7, 20–22, 32, 77, 79, 99–100, 102, 104, 145–147, 150, 160–164, 166–168, 180, 182–183, 186, 188, 190–194, 196–198
United Kingdom 111, 147, 160, 166, 168, 177, 193–194, 197
United Nations 77
  Special Commission on Iraq 54
United States,
  arms control policy 121
  House Permanent Select Committee on Intelligence 64
  intelligence 53, 65, 133, 136, 146
  National Security Strategy 101
  nuclear doctrine/posture 71, 148, 167, 169, 175–177, 180
  nuclear triad 4, 8, 12, 15, 32, 83–85, 106, 115, 119, 174
  nuclear umbrella 21, 166, 182
  "Zero Option" position 52, 61
U.S. Air Force 4, 82, 106
U.S. Arms Control and Disarmament Agency (ACDA) 64–66
U.S. Congress 53, 133, 136–137, 161, 175
  Congressional Budget Office 4
U.S. Department of Defense 106, 196
U.S. National Security Council (NSC) 195, 196
U.S. Navy 88, 149
U.S. Nuclear Posture Review (NPR) xxii–xxiv, 58
  2002 181
  2010 181
  2018 22–23, 26, 181, 183
  2020 167
  2022 182
U.S. Senate Armed Services Committee 14
U.S. State Department 99, 161
U.S. Strategic Command xxiii, 3, 82, 87–88
USSR/Soviets 4–7, 10–11, 17, 19, 25–27, 30, 32, 34, 44, 49–52, 57–58, 61–62, 70–72, 103–105, 107, 111, 116, 118–120, 150–152, 161, 183
  collapse of 7
  doctrine regarding use of nuclear weapons 71
Ustinov, Dmitry 104

V

Valdai Discussion Club 58, 169, 172
Vanunu, Mordechai 140
Verizon 16, 19
Vietnam War 6, 148, 163
Volkel Air Force Base 149
Votkinsk missile plant 52, 104–105

W

W-76-2 low-yield nuclear warhead xxiv, 149
warhead "sponge" 83, 84
Washington Post viii
Washington Spectator viii, 15
Weapons Intelligence, Nonproliferation and Arms Control Center (WINPAC) 65
Weapons of Mass Destruction (WMD) viii, 23, 64–66, 122, 136, 147, 182
West Bank xiv
World War II 9, 30, 138
Wyoming 3, 83

Y

Yang Chengjun 61
Yeltsin, Boris 11, 62
Yugoslavia 7
Yuzhnoye 104

Z
Zakharova, Maria 100
Zelensky, Volodymyr 145–146, 150, 193–194
Zhao Tong 117

Praise for *Highway to Hell*

"Dante Alighieri described a fictional Perdition in *The Inferno*. Scott Ritter knows that failure to put down nuclear weapons truly sets us on *The Highway to Hell*. An urgent read requiring urgent action."

—DENNIS J. KUCINICH, Former U.S. Congressman and 2004, 2008 Democratic candidate for President

"No one knows more about nuclear weapons than Scott Ritter. He has devoted the better part of his post-military career to warning the world about the dangers of their use and how close we are at this writing to universal destruction. The keys to universal destruction were created by the American Empire, mimicked by its selected allies, stolen by the Israelis who time and again have threatened to destroy the world, and now rests in the hands of dangerous immoral people. In *Highway to Hell,* Scott shares his vast knowledge of these horrible weapons and whispers into our ears a warning: If someone repeatedly threatens to destroy the planet and has the means to do so, you better take them seriously. Don't expect to get much sleep once you've started to read this book."

HON. ANDREW P. NAPOLITANO, Former NJ Superior Court Judge, *NY Times* best-selling author

"Scott Ritter has done it again. Another great read. As a former Command Chief of Space Command, the command which had the responsibility of our land based nuclear arsenal, I have seen up close what nuclear weapons can do. I think we should take heed to what Scott has documented. Anyone who cares about the survival of our planet should read this remarkable chronicle."

DENNIS FRITZ, Director, Eisenhower Media Network and former Command Chief of Space Command

"Sadly, many world leaders have lost the necessary fear of nuclear war. Scott's writings help us understand how hard work and organizing by regular people can change the direction of international policy. His journey is relevant to the struggle that we all experience and reading about it will surely motivate you to do your part."

GARLAND NIXON, Host, *NewsViews with Garland Nixon*

More Praise for *Highway to Hell*

"Scott Ritter's *Highway to Hell* is an accessible must-read chronicle on the biggest existential question facing humanity: the threat of nuclear conflict. This book takes us on a journey that empowers readers not only with the history and geopolitical analysis we need to understand the problem, but also the steps we must take to stop imperial madness before it's too late."

DANNY HAIPHONG, Host, *The Left Lens with Danny Haiphong* podcast